Junk for Joy!

SIÂN BERRY

Junk for Joy!

OVER 50 PROJECTS
TO INSPIRE YOU TO
RE-USE AND RECYCLE

PHOTOGRAPHY BY SARAH CUTTLE
KYLE BOOKS LIMITED

To Mum, Dad and every BBC *Blue Peter* project I ever tried.

First published in Great Britain in 2011 by
Kyle Books Limited
23, Howland Street
London W1T 4AY
general.enquiries@kylebooks.com
www.kylebooks.com

ISBN: 978 1 85626 973 5

A CIP catalogue record for this title is available from the British Library

Siân Berry is hereby identified as the author of this work in accordance with Section 77 of the Copyright, Designs and Patents Act 1988.

Text © Siân Berry 2011
Photographs © Sarah Cuttle 2011
Design © Kyle Books Limited 2011

Editor: Vicky Orchard
Design: Turnbull Grey
Photography: Sarah Cuttle
Copy editor: Barbara Bonser
Production: Nic Jones and Sheila Smith

Colour reproduction by Sang Choy in Singapore
Printed in China by 1010 Printing International Ltd

Note to readers
The author and publisher have taken great care to ensure the information in this book is accurate. However, the advice provided will not be suitable for every situation, and your own circumstances, materials, tools and requirements will vary. Your own judgement, and an assessment of your skills are all vital. In different countries and territories, regulations governing work that can be carried out by non-qualified persons will also vary. If in any doubt, professional help and advice should always be sought. Neither the author nor the publisher of this work can assume any responsibility for loss, damage or injury incurred as a result of relying on the accuracy of the information given.

CONTENTS

Introduction

What do I mean by junk? I mean household or personal items that risk being thrown out because they are past their best, at the end of their useful life or just not wanted.

I also mean things you can pick up free or very cheaply from tips and reclamation yards, junk shops, charity shops, thrift shops, internet recycling services, from friends and family members or simply at the side of the street.

Junk can be ugly; out-of-style homewares or beaten up, worn and cracked items that need repairs. It can also be beautiful; like the old kitchen and farm tools that line the walls of rustic bars and restaurants, or the reclaimed chimney pots in my garden.

Junk can be full of history and interest; an old cupboard passed down through a family or the photographer's show-cards I picked up in a shop in Brighton, showing mysterious ladies from a century ago in their Sunday best.

Above all, junk should be a starting point; a springboard for ideas and the inspiration for revamps, stylish remakes and new creations that are all your own.

What do I mean by joy? I mean the joy of making new things for your home and garden – or unique gifts for others – that aren't expensive, bland chain-store clones, but exactly the way you want them with absolutely no compromise on style.

I also mean the joy of working with your hands; the satisfaction of being creative, putting your ideas into practice and gaining new skills and abilities in the process.

If you read the stories of other junk fiends that are included in these pages you will see how much pride and satisfaction you can get from a junk project that bears fruit. This feeling, combined with my incurable sentimentality (which makes me want to 'save' everything from the landfill site) is what keeps me happily recycling the junk I find.

Above all, junk should be a starting point; a springboard for ideas.

And if that isn't enough, by saving resources in this way you'll also be doing excellent work on behalf of the world's environment. And who could argue with that?

This book isn't your average 'how to' guide. The main aim of this book is to inspire, not to instruct you how to make pieces identical to mine. As well as a wide range of great ideas for inside the home, I've taken on some outdoors projects, and others to impress and delight children.

While reading about these projects, I hope you will have many more ideas for creating things of your own from the junk you find. And, above all, I hope it inspires you to get as much joy from your junk as I do!

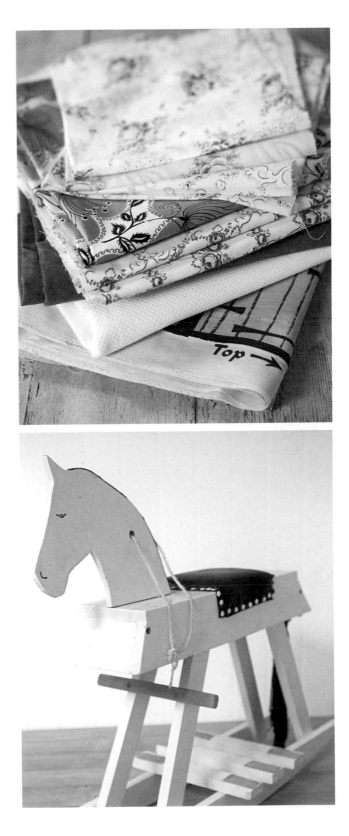

1

Simple
spruce-ups

Simple spruce-ups

This chapter shows how to restore items made from wood, melamine, metal and pottery in different styles and colours. These simple spruce-ups will take pieces that are just a little bit tired or old and give them a new look and another lease of life.

Here, I've focused on different ways to restore or change the surfaces of furnishings and accessories. Sometimes a quick and simple change, such as a fresh coat of paint or new handles, can transform an item completely.

Pieces suitable for these projects may be things you already own or items from friends, family, charity shops, junk shops or just objects left out in the street for people to take away. As long as an item is structurally intact, it's a candidate for one of these projects, and even broken garden pots can be revamped using the textured paint technique on page 24.

If a large item, such as a sideboard or table, is scratched or damaged, deciding to restore its whole surface can be daunting. When I first started out, I used to worry that I might get things wrong or make a mess but, with a few simple techniques, getting a professional-looking finish turned out to be much easier than I imagined.

The whole process of sanding and oiling a wooden table can be done in less than a day, and if you use quick-drying acrylic gloss and a roller to add a new paint finish, a weekend is all you need to restore even a large cupboard.

And you don't have to restrict yourself to plain colours and flat surfaces. I also show how to use découpage for a more creative, decorative finish that will bring out your artistic side.

Once you have these simple techniques in your repertoire, they can be applied to a whole range of projects, enabling you to restore, change and update items again and again with different looks.

Kitchen cupboard revamp

I found this beaten-up cupboard unit in a local junk shop. It had been taken from a kitchen and was on sale for next to nothing. But under layers of yellowing paint it was made of solid wood, so I could see it had potential. Here I'll show how you can use vintage door handles and a lick of paint to revamp similar pieces of neglected or thrown away furniture.

What you'll need

Cupboard unit
Screwdriver and screws
Paint stripper
Protective gloves and glasses
Scraper
Rough and smooth grades of sandpaper and sanding block
Wood filler and kitchen knife
Masking tape
Water-based wood primer
Paint brushes – large and small
Water-based gloss paint
Small gloss rollers and tray
White spirit and rags
Wood stain, Danish oil and rags
Wire wool
Soft polishing cloth
Hammer and a nail
Replacement door or drawer handles

1. Start by unscrewing and removing any old handles and fittings from your furniture. This may leave holes and other marks, but you can always fill these later.

2. Then, move on to restoring the finish. If you want to strip several layers of paint from any parts of your furniture (such as the wooden work surface for my kitchen unit) you'll need to use paint stripper. See page 21 for details of how to use this chemical – and for some important safety notes about its use.

3. Underneath old painted finishes, you may find wood that's very scratched or discoloured. If so, sand it thoroughly with rough 'paint stripping grade' sandpaper. Sand painted surfaces firmly using a sanding block, to provide a fresh surface for priming and painting.

4. Now fill any cracks, dents and holes caused by wear and tear, or by removing fittings such as handles. Apply wood filler with a kitchen knife, then sand it smooth once it has set hard. Match the colour of your filler to the wood in areas where you aren't going to apply paint.

5. Next, protect other parts with masking tape and apply primer to all the painted surfaces using a brush. Leave to dry for a few hours.

6. After lightly sanding the primer to remove brush marks, apply three coats of gloss paint with the roller, sanding with very fine paper between coats. For parts that the roller can't reach, such as the inside edges of the door panels, use a small paint brush.

7. To finish off the unpainted wooden parts, use masking tape to protect your newly painted surfaces, then sand the wood smooth using a series of gradually finer sandpaper grades. Always sand in the direction of the wood grain to achieve the best finish.

8. The next step is to apply wood stain, which will darken the wood and help to disguise any remaining marks. Wipe this on with a rag in the direction of the grain. For parts with the end-grain of the wood exposed, you should dilute the stain with some Danish oil because these will soak up the stain much more easily. Also apply the stain to any wooden parts of your door handles.

9. Finish off the wooden parts with two thick applications of Danish oil, leaving each application to dry for a couple of hours, then smoothing with wire wool between coats. Then, once all the oil has soaked in, polish the surface to a sheen with a soft cloth.

10. Finally, fit the new handles to your furniture. I made a pilot hole for each screw with a hammer and nail, then used screws to attach my reclaimed handles.

For my unit, I chose acrylic, water-based gloss to reduce the drying time and used a small foam roller to apply the paint. This leaves a lovely 'stippled' surface without brush marks that is very tough. The trick is to apply it in several thin coats and to run the roller very lightly over the surfaces – without applying too much pressure – when finishing off each coat. This removes the lines made by the edges of the roller and leaves the finish virtually flawless.

Another way to update a cupboard

One of the perils (or benefits!) of making things for yourself is the temptation to re-do things just because you fancy a change.

I did love the simple wooden look of my first revamp, but I had also found another gorgeous set of vintage door handles in powder blue, so I decided to change the style of the cupboard to match these with another mini project. Because I already had a good paint finish to start with, this was very easy to do and took only a few hours.

1. Start by removing the handles you want to replace, fill the holes with wood filler, then sand, prime and retouch the paint on the relevant parts of the cupboard.

2. To paint the inside panels of cupboard doors, as I have done here, use masking tape to protect the outer frames of the doors, pressing it down very carefully around the edges. Then use a gloss roller to apply two coats of contrasting paint to the inner panels.

3. After that, use a small, artist's brush to paint the inner edges, being careful to brush away from the masking tape. Despite this, when the tape is removed, a few tiny leaks may have spread onto the outer frame of the door so touch these up by hand to get a clean line.

4. Finally, add your new handles. The ones I used needed a screw fitting from the inside of the drawers, so I measured up and drilled holes in the correct places before fixing them in place.

And that's it – a new vintage style for a cupboard in just a few steps.

What you'll need
Cupboard unit

Screwdriver

Wood filler and kitchen knife

Sandpaper and sanding block

Wood primer

Gloss paint in suitable colours

Masking tape

Small gloss roller and tray

Artist's paint brush

Vintage door handles

Measuring tape or ruler

Pencil

Drill and wood drill bits

It was easy to change the look of this unit simply by adding coloured panels and some vintage handles.

Repaint a metal lamp stand

Enamel paints, and other paints intended for metal, are designed specifically to prevent brush marks from showing and so can give a really smooth and professional finish. They are ideal for simple revamps of pieces like this metal lamp stand.

What you'll need

Metal lamp stand

Sandpaper or coarse wire wool

Masking tape

Quick-drying enamel paint or metal paint – look for brands that boast about their smooth finish

A good quality paint brush – a large artist's brush or small varnish brush is ideal

White spirit

Tissues

You can also use the same technique on small wooden or ceramic pieces, so why not paint several items at a time to create a colour-matched set of accessories for a room?

1. A good starting surface is needed for a really smooth final coat of paint, so sand down your item (if it's wood) or use coarse wire wool for metal or ceramic pieces. An existing enamel finish may have chips, so smooth these out with sandpaper before finishing with wire wool.

2. Before painting, protect lamp fittings and wires with masking tape. Press the tape down carefully at the edges to help prevent leaks.

3. The paint needs to be applied in two or three thin coats, but don't make these too thin, or you will see brush marks as the paint builds up. It's best to use a fully loaded brush to cover a large area quickly and to try not to over-brush. Once you've completed a coat, check for any drips and blobs of paint at corners and edges, and brush these out before they dry.

4. Once the final coat is finished, remove the masking tape. Any leaks that have spread under the tape onto plastic or metal parts can be scraped off or removed carefully with white spirit and the corner of a folded tissue.

Wooden folding dining table

A folding wooden table is a multi-purpose piece of furniture. Use it as an expanding dining table, a desk or as a fold-out surface for a sewing machine or craft project. Most of the tables you can find in second-hand shops are made of solid or veneered wood and are very inexpensive, but not always in great condition. My table was covered in ugly, scratched, dark varnish, but I could tell the wood underneath was lovely so I decided to give it a quick and easy makeover.

Getting the old varnish off is the first task for a project like this. It's a very messy job that is best done outside, protecting the ground with a sheet and plenty of newspaper.

1. Wearing protective gloves and glasses, start by applying a thick layer of paint stripper to the table. Dab the jelly-like chemical on with a brush, then wait a few minutes for the varnish to blister. Add more stripper on top of the first layer, pushing it well into any grooves with the paint brush. After 20 minutes (during which you should watch for any areas drying out and apply more stripper if needed) the dissolved varnish can be scraped away onto pieces of newspaper, wrapped up and disposed of carefully.

What you'll need
Wooden dining table
Newspaper and sheet to protect the ground
Protective gloves and glasses
Paint stripper
Paint brush
Scraper
Coarse wire wool
White spirit
Medium and fine grades of sandpaper and sanding block
Danish oil and lots of old, soft rags
Reclaimed door handles
Screwdriver and screws or bolts

Safety note
Paint stripper can burn your skin or eyes, so wear rubber gloves and glasses or goggles when using this product.

2. After scraping away the varnish, use coarse wire wool dipped in white spirit to scrub away any remaining specks and clean away the residue of the paint stripper.

Repeat steps 1 and 2 for all parts of the table, working on one section at a time.

3. Next comes sanding. Work in the direction of the grain and cover every surface of the table. In areas with deeper scratches, use coarser grades of sandpaper to smooth these out before finishing off with a finer grade. My table was relatively unscratched, so one round of medium sandpaper, followed by a finer grade, was enough.

4. The last step for an attractive, durable wood finish is to apply Danish oil. Using oil is an excellent way to protect wooden furniture. It is much easier to look after than varnish, which is easily scratched and hard to retouch. Instead, wood oils soak into the wood grain to protect it, and the surface can be polished to a nice subtle sheen rather than a high shine. To apply the oil, pour it in a pool in the middle of each top panel of your table, then rub it in thoroughly with a rag. For vertical surfaces, such as the legs, pour a little oil onto a rag and smear it on instead. Two or three applications of oil are enough to protect your table; leave it to soak in for a few hours between applications.

5. Last of all, buff the whole piece with a dry, soft cloth and fix any new handles to doors and drawers using screws or bolts, as appropriate.

Paint stripper is a very strong, jelly-like solvent, which is applied to a surface with a brush in order to dissolve paint or varnish without harming the wood underneath. It's important it doesn't dry out during this process as this will prevent the old varnish being scraped away. Therefore, it's a good idea to do paint stripping in stages, working on about one square metre of wood at a time.

Co-ordinated garden pots

Brighten up your garden with this simple project. Starting with a range of differently shaped and coloured terracotta pots, you can create an attractive co-ordinated look just by mixing sand with ordinary gloss paint. I have used pots painted in two bold colours to make an attractive display, which looks great with flowering plants or foliage. This finish won't be weatherproof forever, but still looks good when it has developed a few chips and flakes and it doesn't take long to reapply when needed.

What you'll need
Terracotta pots
Newspaper or sheet to protect the ground
Disposable container
Water-based gloss paint
Tablespoon
Builder's sand
Paint brush
Stones or strips of wood

1. First, spread the newspaper or sheet on the ground and clean the pots to remove any dirt and dust that might stop the paint from sticking.

2. Then, in a disposable container, mix together a good amount of paint with a couple of tablespoons of the sand.

3. Use an ordinary brush to apply the paint, first with a brushing action, then dabbing all over the surface to distribute the sand more evenly.

4. You will find the textured finish is a bit patchy after the first coat, but don't worry about this. Adding a second coat of sandy paint after the first has dried will fill in any gaps.

5. While the paint dries, prop the pots up on stones or strips of wood, to prevent them sticking to the newspaper or sheet.

This little revamp is so easy you could repaint in a different colour scheme every year!

Because the sand may be slightly damp, it's best to use water-based paint, so they will mix together easily. Even so, while you are painting, you will need to stir the paint around every so often, as the heavy sand will sink to the bottom of the container.

Junk Fiends: Dave & Debbie Powell

Making things for this book has sent me to a variety of places looking for junk, from reclamation yards to charity shops and car boot sales. In order for people like me to re-use junk, someone needs to have saved it from a landfill in the first place; and that's where Dave and Debbie Powell come in.

Based in the south of England, the Bracknell Re-use Project is a one-stop shop where people can donate unwanted items and find treasures to re-use or remake. Working with a local network of traders (for example, a non-profit organisation that provides inexpensive furniture to those in need) Dave and Debbie will collect items from local people for free and then begin to work out the best way to re-use, repair or recycle them.

When I visited the project, Dave explained how the idea came out of their existing business restoring and re-selling collectables and hi-fi equipment.

'Green Home Electronics is a great business because there is a steady supply of equipment and I have the skills to fix the stuff. We started with antiques in 2004, but the project soon outgrew the house after we moved into electronics. We now rent two units in an old stable block.

'Basically, I love toys –
anything that works I
like to mess around with,
so I'm ideal for this job.'

'One of these units is now dedicated to re-use, and is filling up fast with an eclectic range of junk and collectables.'

Being multi-skilled has helped Dave to widen the range of items the pair can take in: 'As well as being an electronic engineer I also trained as an apprentice at the Royal Aircraft Establishment and have always loved working on engines. Basically, I love toys – anything that works I like to mess around with, so I'm ideal for this job.'

Debbie's motivation is more about saving resources: 'It's the green issue. I don't like to see waste. I really want to see things put back to use and I get a big kick when people come in looking for a particular hi-fi because it was the model their dad used to have. And, rather than the equipment going into landfill, it'll now go to someone who will really treasure it.'

Dave says the need for the re-use project became clear when recycling regulations were changed: 'There used to be people who would keep the local dump tidy and – in return – be allowed to pick up and re-use things. But, with new rules on dumping electrical items, that tradition died out.

'Now, when things are recycled, they're sent to centralised plants where they are broken down into raw materials, which is a huge waste of equipment that could still be used. Our aim is to be there to stop things getting near the tips in the first place.'

The project is forging a local network of people from different charities and businesses to take the items they collect. 'One of the things we're really keen to do is think and act locally,' says Dave. 'It's so that we don't just help the environment but also the economy in our area. We do want to make money and provide value to our customers, but it's just as important that we provide value to the environment and value to the community where we live.'

'It's the green issue. I don't like to see waste. I really want to see things put back to use and I get a big kick when people come in looking for a particular hi-fi because it was the model their dad used to have.'

Cover a table top with découpage

I found this old-fashioned melamine, gold-edged table that had potential. Its tapered black legs were a lovely shape so I decided to cover the surface with a patchwork of paper, which I cut from a musical score, using a simple technique called découpage.

Découpage is a process of gluing on layers of cut-out pieces of paper, often with motifs laid on top of a background pattern, followed by many layers of varnish that seal down the edges and create a durable finish.

What you'll need
An old table
Sandpaper and sanding block
Paper cut into pieces (pages of a book or magazine are ideal)
Scissors
A mixture of PVA (wood or craft) glue and water
Brushes
Varnish
Enamel paint (for feet)
Sticky tack and pencils or sticks of wood

1. Clean and prepare the surface of your table with a light sanding.

2. Prepare lots of pieces of paper. It is easiest to make a random, overlapping pattern (where the pieces vary in size and shape). However, if you were very careful, you could also aim for a more regular pattern.

   I created differently shaped pieces from the pages of my musical score by cutting between the musical staves. If you use a book or magazine, cutting out separate columns or paragraphs would work well too.

3. Water down some PVA glue in a bowl. A ratio of about 1.5 parts water to one part of glue is about right mixture.

4. In the area where you want to start, brush a layer of glue mixture onto the surface, then brush more glue over both sides of a piece of paper.

5. Place a corner of the paper on the surface, then brush it down flat from the corner to minimise wrinkles in the paper (some small wrinkles will probably still appear afterwards, but these will reduce a lot as the glue dries).

6. Repeat the two steps above to lay down new pieces of paper, overlapping each one until you have covered the whole surface.

7. You will need to wrap the paper around edges and corners. For these areas, allow the glue to soak right into the paper first, so that it becomes really soft and flexible. It can also help to cut thinner or smaller pieces for these parts to reduce the amount of folding.

8. Let the glue dry for about 6-8 hours, then check for any gaps, mistakes or large creases. Sanding down a bump then covering with another piece of paper will help make the surface nearly perfect, ready for varnishing.

9. Once the glue is thoroughly dry, cover the whole surface with several coats of varnish. I used a water-based acrylic varnish that would resist yellowing. It also dried quickly, so I only had to wait a few hours between each coat. For a smooth finish on large areas, apply lots of thin coats, brushing each one in a different direction.

10. To finish off my table, I removed the metal coverings from the bottom of the legs and painted them with black enamel paint. To make painting these fiddly little pieces easier, I put sticky tack inside and supported them on sticks.

For chair legs and other thin parts, long, narrow strips of paper wrapped around in a spiral pattern can look really good.

2

Creative ways
with small items

Creative ways with small items

This chapter is all about remaking and restoring junk into smaller household accessories, including picture frames, placemats, glassware, vases, bowls and letter racks. I've tried to use items that any of us can easily lay our hands on around the home and garden, from empty wine bottles and corks to natural 'junk', such as driftwood and leaves.

These are projects to suit any home, and many are adaptable to suit your own tastes. For example, if you don't like the look of my stylish Italian ladies from the 1950s, use the same technique and choose a different kind of magazine cover and the placemats project on page 63 will become uniquely yours.

The projects in this chapter show you how to recycle a wide range of junk in new ways. A dirty and broken wooden draining rack is transformed into a letter rack for a hallway; bamboo steamers become beautiful tealight shades for parties; picture frames are given a new lease of life with beads, driftwood, glitter and slate; and placemats are customised with wallpaper or pages from magazines.

I've also tested and adapted some classic recycling ideas to come up with new ways of using vinyl records, wine bottles and corks.

All of these projects can be completed in one weekend and most of them will take no more than a couple of hours from start to finish. Many of them would also be a good starting point for a complete beginner with no knowledge of DIY.

There are important safety notes accompanying some of these projects, especially the ones that use broken glass, sharp knives and hot plastic. However, the simple cutting and gluing techniques involved in making placemats, tealight shades and the cork memo board are also easy and safe enough to be completed by or with older children.

Letter rack from dish drainer

This drainer lasted a very long time in my kitchen, but eventually became too wobbly to hold plates and pots safely. After securing it with wire for a year, I gave up and replaced it, but decided to recycle one of the racks to hold letters, postcards and keys in the hallway.

What you'll need
Wooden draining rack

Hacksaw

Sandpaper and metal file

Paint brushes

Wood primer/undercoat

Water-based gloss paint in two contrasting colours

A scrap piece of wood, plywood or fibreboard

Drill

Screws and screwdriver

Large, screw-in hooks

1. After dismantling the drainer, trim the pieces with a hacksaw to get a neat ladder shape.

2. Now sand down the wood with coarse sandpaper. To remove any build-up of limescale or dirt from the inside edges of the struts, use a metal file or sandpaper wrapped around a thin scrap of wood or a pencil.

3. Using a small paint brush, prime the wood. Reaching every surface can be tricky, and it's easy to miss a few corners, so this is best done in a number of stages, turning the rack to face a different way each time.

4. After priming, follow up with two to three coats of gloss paint. Be careful that drips don't build on the reverse side when painting between the slats. It's a good idea to turn the piece over to check once you've finished a side, brushing away any blobs of paint before they dry.

5. Now prepare the base. Use any scrap of sheet material you have to hand (I used a thick piece of fibreboard left over from making a desk). Cut this to the same size as the rack, then sand, prime and paint it in a contrasting colour.

6. The rack needs to be attached firmly to the base with screws. So that these don't split the wooden struts of the rack, drill small holes first.

7. Finally, add some large screw-in hooks at the bottom of the rack to hang keys and other items. These can also split the wood, so drill tiny holes before screwing them in by hand.

When several coats of paint are needed on a project a quick-drying water-based gloss paint saves time and is better for the environment too!

Ideas to update picture frames

No picture frame – no matter how out of style – should ever be thrown away. There are so many different ways you can revamp them to fit in with your home. And even when the glass breaks, there are plenty of ways to re-use the outer parts of the frame. See the cork memo board project on page 46 for just one idea.

What you'll need:
Picture frame
Bricks, newspaper or protective sheet
Spray paint or gloss enamel
Paint brushes
PVA (wood or craft) glue
Glitter
Clear acrylic varnish

Here are four simple ways to restyle picture frames, which I hope will inspire you to come up with many more ideas of your own.

Glue on some glitter

Covering anything in a thick, even layer of glitter can be laborious, but here's an easy way to get the same effect without using industrial quantities of glitter.

1. Remove the frame's glass and backing and place the frame between supports (such as bricks) above a newspaper or protective sheet.

2. Spray or paint the frame with a base colour that matches your glitter. This helps to make even a thin layer of glitter look effective.

3. Once the paint is dry, place a piece of folded newspaper in a 'V' shape between the frame and the supports. The fold will collect spare glitter during each application, which can then be poured back into its container and re-used.

4. Brush a thick layer of wood glue onto the frame, then sprinkle glitter all over it, tapping the side of the container to release small amounts of glitter at a time in a steady flow. For the non-vertical edges, pick up some spare glitter from the fold in the newspaper and push this gently onto the frame with your fingers.

5. While the glue is still wet, repeat this process several times, removing the newspaper, pouring the glitter out of the fold before replacing the newspaper below the frame and sprinkling again.

6. Once almost all the glitter is sticking to the frame. press it down lightly and leave the glue to dry. (Clean your hands so you don't press on the glitter with sticky fingers that will end up pulling it off instead!)

7. Once the glue is completely dry it will change from white to clear and the frame will be completely covered with glitter. The last step is to apply a thick coat of acrylic varnish, dabbing it on lightly with a brush. This will help stop the glitter from shedding when the frame is handled, and also makes the whole thing extra shiny.

Embellish with beads
These beads, from a collection of junk-shop jewellery, look really pretty on a picture frame (see overleaf). I also painted the frame in a complementary base colour. Epoxy glue is strong, but this frame still needs careful handling when finished. If any beads do break off, a drop of extra glue can be used to fix them on again.

What you'll need
Picture frame
Paint and brushes for a base coat
Epoxy **resin** glue
Reclaimed beads from old or broken jewellery
Tweezers

---

1. Remove the glass and backing from the frame, then paint the frame in a suitable base colour. Any spare acrylic, emulsion, enamel or gloss paint is suitable for this project.

2. Mix up a large quantity of epoxy resin glue, place the frame on a tray to catch stray beads, then spread a layer of glue about 2mm thick over the front face of the frame.

3. Pop all your beads into a container. You will need to work quite quickly, as the glue will set in about 15 minutes (don't buy a quick-setting brand of epoxy for this job!). Start by sprinkling on the beads randomly. To fill in any gaps, use tweezers to pick up and push beads into the spaces.

4. If any gaps remain at the end of this process, you can simply mix up more epoxy and use the tweezers to dip individual beads into the glue and place them on the frame.

Decorate with driftwood

I have decorated a plain wooden frame with slices cut from a piece of driftwood that I picked up on a coastal walk.

What you'll need
Driftwood
Tenon saw or hacksaw
Sandpaper and sanding block
Danish oil or clear acrylic varnish
PVA (wood or craft) glue
Picture frame

1. Cut thinnish sections from your pieces of driftwood using a fine-toothed saw (a tenon saw is ideal for this job) to reduce the amount of sanding needed afterwards.

2. Sanding the thin slices can be a bit fiddly. Hold them flat using sticky tack or clamp a few at a time in a vice. You can then use a sanding block to smooth them down gently.

3. Once one side of each piece has been sanded smooth, apply a small amount of Danish oil to bring out the pattern of circles in the wood grain. Alternatively, you can varnish them with clear acrylic varnish. Only treat the sanded side, so that the slices will stick properly to the frame.

4. Then, simply glue the pieces to your frame, applying a big blob of wood glue to each piece before pressing down.

Glass frame decorated with slate

Plain glass 'clip' frames are ideal for decorating in interesting ways. You could paint a pattern using clear craft paints (as used for the front door panel of the doll's house on page 176), or stick almost anything around the edges of the glass to frame a smaller picture or postcard.

A broken roof tile is perfect for breaking up into small, thin pieces suitable for this project.

1. Wearing protective glasses in case of flying chips of slate, break your roof tile into pieces by resting it on top of two bricks placed slightly apart and hitting it sharply with a hammer. Repeat this process to break the slate into progressively smaller and thinner pieces.

What you'll need

Protective eyewear
A spare or broken slate roofing tile
Bricks
Hammer
Glass 'clip' frame
Epoxy resin glue

2. Then, collect up the slate pieces and work out an attractive way to arrange these around your frame. It's a good idea to plan this before mixing your glue, so you can attach them all in one session before the glue sets hard (you'll have about 15 minutes after mixing the resin before this happens).

3. Remove the backing from the glass, noting where the clips are located and apply the glue to the back of each piece of slate before sticking the pieces in place one by one.

4. Once the glue is dry, turn the glass over (being careful to handle it by the long edges, not the ends or corners) place your picture in the centre and reattach the backing with the frame's metal clips.

Memo board from wine corks

Wine bottle corks have a habit of accumulating around the house in drawers and bowls. They might be useful one day to stop a bottle but you don't need dozens for that, so why not turn them into this simple memo board?

What you'll need

Corks (about 60 corks were enough for the size of board shown opposite)

Hacksaw and a cutting surface

Sandpaper and a sanding block

Tray

Measuring tape

A spare piece of wood or board

Brightly coloured paint – gloss, emulsion or acrylic

Paint brushes, including a small, stiff brush for glue

Pieces of an old picture frame, or any kind of wooden strip material

PVA (wood or craft) glue

Screws and screwdriver

I've cut the corks in cross-section, so that the exposed ends show a lovely range of colours, including some stained with red wine. I also found a few larger corks, which I used to make an interesting, irregular pattern.

1. Corks are soft and easy to cut. Use a small hacksaw and a cutting board to slice each one in half, then cut each of the pieces in half again. Whole corks vary slightly in length but, once cut into quarters, the difference will be very small. Any pieces that are much longer than the others can always be sanded down.

2. Arrange the cork pieces on a tray to see what size frame you'll need, then prepare the base and edges of the frame.

3. Any kind of sheet material will do for the base – wood or board is ideal. Cut it to size, then paint it with a bright colour that contrasts with the corks. Patches of this colour will show through the corks on the finished board.

4. Now add a frame. You could reclaim an old picture frame for this, cutting the pieces down if needed, or cut pieces with 45 degree corners from any suitable strips of wood you have available. Here, I used the beading from the inside frame of an old door.

The frame of this memo board was made from pieces of the wooden door used for the tiled table project on page 84. To cut the corners accurately at 45 degrees, I made my own mitre template from a spare piece of wood with hardboard attached at the correct angle.

5. Glue the pieces of frame onto the painted base with wood glue or screw them on from the reverse side.

6. The final step is to glue down the pieces of cork. Use a brush to apply a blob of wood glue to each piece before placing into the frame (this is much stronger than applying a layer of glue to the base). It's hard to make a completely regular pattern of rows so, instead, make the pattern deliberately irregular and interesting by including a few larger slices from sparkling wine or champagne corks.

Leafy tealight shades

Bamboo steamers are cheap to buy and great for cooking healthy dishes, but unfortunately they don't last forever. Eventually, they always fall apart. It's environmentally friendly to chop up the pieces and put them in the compost, but why not try this cute way to re-use some of the parts first?

These tealight shades, made from kitchen greaseproof paper and fresh leaves, won't last forever either but they look really pretty and take just minutes to make. One set of steamers can provide parts for a whole batch – perfect to decorate your garden or terrace for a party.

Square shade

1. Start by selecting four flat bamboo sticks that are about the same length. Measure a suitable height for the paper walls, leaving about 1cm of stick at either end.

2. Then decide how long to make each side of the square: somewhere between about 8cm and 12cm is a good size. Cut out a piece of kitchen greaseproof paper that measures four times this length (plus an extra 1cm for overlap) and twice the height measured in step 1.

3. Fold the paper in half along its length, then unfold it and mark at 8–12 cm intervals along the bottom edge to show where each of the sticks will need to be placed, starting flush against one edge.

4. Next, spray a thin layer of glue onto the bottom half of the paper, below the fold.

5. The next step is to take the leaves and arrange them on the glue-covered paper, making sure that each side of the shade will have a pretty leaf pattern showing through. It's not a problem if some of the leaves overlap the points where the sticks will be placed, but try to avoid putting any thick stems at these points, as they will make the paper hard to fold.

6. Spray another thin layer of glue over the whole area, to cover the top surfaces of the leaves, then carefully fold down the top part of the paper, smoothing it out to prevent large creases. Don't worry about a few small creases, as they won't ruin the finished effect. If the bottom edge is uneven, trim it straight with scissors.

7. The spray glue sticks instantly, so you can move straight on with adding the four sticks of bamboo. Apply a thin layer of PVA glue to each stick with a spatula before placing at the marked point. For a shade that won't wobble, it's important to make sure that the bottom points of all four sticks line up exactly. Placing a straight piece of card on your work surface as a guide helps with this.

8. Leave the wood glue to dry for a short time (why not prepare more shades while you wait?).

9. Once everything has set, you can construct the shade. Fold the four corners along each of the sticks, then trim the free edge so that it tucks neatly into the first corner. Apply a line of glue to the end of the paper and press it into this corner to create the final shape.

Circular shade

This takes a little longer to complete because the circular supports need to be glued securely before use. It's a good idea to prepare several of these circular pieces before making the shades.

1. For the circles, take some thin, broad, curved strips of bamboo from the walls of the steamer and bend them gently into shape. Apply wood glue to the join then, to prevent it springing apart while the glue sets, wrap masking tape tightly around the overlap and leave this in place for several hours.

2. To make the cylindrical body of the shade, start by measuring the circumference of your bamboo circle. A good way to do this is to mark a point on the circle and roll it along a ruler or tape measure.

3. Then select three bamboo sticks that are about the same length and measure a suitable height for the paper that will leave about 1cm of stick at the bottom and – this time – 2cm at the top to allow space for the circle.

4. Next, cut out a piece of greaseproof paper that measures twice this height, with a width that is the circumference of the circle plus 1cm for overlap. Also mark the point where the exact circumference measurement lies.

5. In the same way as for the square shade, fold the paper and use spray glue to stick fresh leaves between the two layers.

6. Next, glue on the bamboo sticks, starting with one at the left hand edge of the paper and adding the other two at equal intervals up to the circumference mark, leaving around one third of the paper free on the right hand side.

7. Then, make a cylinder by sticking the free end to the first bamboo stick just outside the circumference mark (this will make the cylinder just a bit larger than the circular support, allowing the circle to be slotted inside the paper).

8. After leaving the glue to set for a few minutes, apply glue around the bottom half of the bamboo circle and slot it into place inside the top of the paper cylinder.

Safety note

It's best to use these shades outdoors, as the greaseproof paper will catch fire if it comes into contact with a candle flame. If it's windy or you want to bring the shades indoors, be sure to place your candles inside another container, such as an empty glass jar.

This idea works with any straight, flat strips of material. Why not try it with wooden disposable chopsticks after dining out?

Upcycling vinyl records

Making scratched or obsolete records into bowls is another vintage idea. PVC 'vinyl' plastic only needs to be heated to about 90ºC before it becomes soft, so I've tried out three different methods for heating and bending records.

And I haven't stopped at bowls for party snacks. The letter rack and bookend projects make great gifts if you choose records to match the tastes and interests of your friends.

Decorative bowls

Using an oven for heating makes the whole record soft and floppy and is ideal for making decorative bowls of different shapes. You can shape the records by hand straight from the oven or press them around the outside of a mould, but I have found the best way of creating an even shape in the few seconds before the vinyl hardens is to press it between two stacking containers with suitable shapes. This method also helps to make sure the bottom of the bowl is nice and flat.

1. Preheat the oven. Place the ovenproof bowl upside down in the centre of the oven shelf.

2. Open all the doors and windows in the room then place a record into the oven on top of the bowl.

> **What you'll need**
> An oven heated to about 150ºC
> An ovenproof bowl, about 10cm high
> Old records – singles or LPs
> Oven gloves
> Two ceramic or plastic bowls that stack closely together, for pressing

3. Wait for approximately 5 minutes, until the record has softened and its edges are visibly sinking down in folds around the ovenproof bowl. While the record is heating up, prepare your stacking containers nearby on a firm surface. The next stage has to be done very efficiently, because the plastic will harden again within a few seconds of being removed from the oven. However, don't worry if you get the shape wrong the first time; you can simply replace the record in the oven, reheat it and start again.

4. Open the oven door and pull out the record. The plastic will be hot, so it is best to use oven gloves, but can be handled for a second or two with bare hands. Place the softened record straight into one of the stacking bowls, making sure it is placed centrally and that none of the edges are folded down. Then, place the second bowl inside the first and press down hard to push the record into shape. After about 10 seconds, remove the finished bowl from the mould.

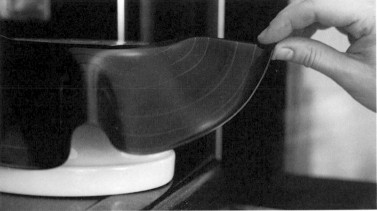

Cooled vinyl is safe but, especially with older records, the plastic may also leach out other chemicals (it was never produced with food safety standards in mind!). Finished bowls and containers are suitable for dry snacks only, and shouldn't be left in contact with any food products for long periods.

Plant holder

For this cute, folded plant holder, heat an LP record in the oven in the same way as for the bowls (see page 52), then create this shape by moulding the softened plastic around an upturned plant pot or drinking glass.

As you will be handling the hot plastic for longer while making this container, be sure to wear protective gloves.

Bookends

Heated vinyl expands slightly when heated in the oven, and this tends to make the edges of the records crinkle up in waves. This is fine for the bowl project, but not if you want to keep parts of your bended project flat and neat. For these bookends, therefore, I used a shallow dish and hot water to heat only the bottom part of the record and to keep the upper part wrinkle free.

This project also needs to be done quickly and efficiently once you've heated the vinyl, so get everything ready before you start.

1. Place a record at an angle against one flat edge of the tray or dish.

2. Pour very hot water into the dish to cover the bottom part of the record.

3. The vinyl will soften immediately. Grab a piece of flat wood and press down onto the record where you want it to bend, pushing up against the corner of the tray or dish to make a straight fold.

4. Then, lie the piece of wood down in the water and press down on it with another piece of scrap wood (avoiding putting your hands in the hot water!). This flattens the bottom part of the record, removing any crinkles.

5. Hold in this position for about 10 seconds to allow the water to cool slightly, then pour in a cup of cold water to harden the vinyl properly.

6. Take the finished bookend out of the water and dry it off. Do this quickly if your record has a paper label, so it doesn't peel off.

Letter rack

The neat bended corners of this letter rack would be impossible to fashion from a fully softened record from the oven. For this project, I've used the concentrated heat of a hairdryer to bend records around large hardback books.

1. Start by placing a record between two heavy books, poking out just where you want the first fold to be made. Put weights on top of the books, or ask a helper to hold them down.

2. With the hairdryer at its fiercest setting, blow heat along the surface of the record, following the line of the books. Move the nozzle back and forth to heat each part evenly.

3. While heating, pull gently upwards at the far edge of the record to feel for when it starts to soften and bend.

4. When you can lift the end easily, turn off the hairdryer and quickly complete the bending process. Use a flat piece of wood or another book to press the raised part firmly against the spine of the book. After a few seconds, the vinyl will be completely hard again.

5. Leave the bottom edge of the record trapped between the books and use the hairdryer to heat the part of the record that runs along the top edge of the upper book. At the same time, press gently forwards on the top of the record until you feel the record start to bend.

6. When it is soft enough, bend the top part of the record right down onto the cover of the book. Use a piece of wood or another book to press against the spine again, to make sure the finished piece will sit flat when made into a rack

7. You will need two or three of these bended pieces for a letter rack. Try folding each one around a book of a different thickness to give dividers of different heights.

8. Finally, mix up some epoxy resin and glue the records together (this makes the rack stronger and more stable) and then attach the records to a base made from any any suitable scrap of wood or board. You shouldn't need to drill any holes; just take thick wood screws and put them through the central holes in the disks.

Cement and glassware centrepiece

I can't resist old coloured glassware. I'd built up this collection of lovely amber-coloured glasses, which looked great but hardly ever got used (I don't often drink strong alcohol or espresso coffee!). To save them from gathering dust on a shelf I put them centre stage by creating a stand to hold both candles and condiments.

What you'll need

A bowl

Vegetable oil

Clingfilm

A small bag of cement

Old glasses or cups

A bucket

Metal spoon

Sandpaper

Paint

Paint brush

---

1. To make sure the cement doesn't stick permanently to the bowl and glassware, cover the inside of the bowl with a layer of vegetable oil. Wrap the glasses in clingfilm and oil this too.

2. Mix the cement in a bucket, following the instructions on the packet to get the correct proportion of powder and water.

3. Scoop the mixture into the oiled bowl and smooth the surface with the back of a metal spoon.

4. Take the wrapped glasses and cups and place them carefully into the cement. I wrapped extra clingfilm around the group of tall glasses, to support them in an upright position.

5. The cement will start to harden quickly as the chemicals in the powder react together. However, wait a while before removing the glasses. The material will take many hours to reach its full strength and the narrow walls between the holes will crumble if you pull out the glasses too soon.

6. Once the cement is properly hard, gently pull out the glasses. They should slide out quite easily, leaving matching holes in the cement.

7. The clingfilm will leave a lightly wrinkled pattern in the sides of the cement wells, so sand these down lightly to make them neater before painting.

8. The cement block also slid cleanly out of my curved bowl for painting. You can use any kind of paint for this job; I chose a metallic shade of blue, painted on thickly.

9. The glasses will now slide easily in and out of the moulded wells for cleaning, and can be used to hold candles, other decorations or seasonings.

After a few experiments, I found that ordinary vegetable oil worked well as a low-tech 'mould release agent' for the cement. To be extra careful with my glasses, I also wrapped them in clingfilm before oiling. This left small crease marks in the hardened cement, but these were easy to smooth down with sandpaper.

Cement is very easy to mix and use. It can be put to use in lots of different craft projects indoors as well as outside.

You can find old magazines in second-hand bookshops, many of which now sell on the internet. This makes it easy to find eye-catching publications to suit your own interests and hobbies.

Personalised placemats

I picked up some old placemats, with dated fox hunting designs, from a charity shop in Wales. They look fantastic now, showing off pages from 1950s Italian fashion magazines. With matching coasters, covered with postcards from the same period, I've made a quirky place-setting that you can copy in any style that suits you.

What you'll need

Placemats and coasters
Old magazines and postcards
Scissors and pencil
Small paint brushes and a good varnish brush
PVA (wood or craft) glue
Heavy books
Enamel paint
Clear acrylic varnish

1. Clean and dry the mats and coasters, to ensure they are free of grease and dust before gluing.

2. Cut the magazine pages slightly larger than the mats, so the paper can be wrapped around the edges. If you are using thicker cardboard, such as the postcards I have used for my coasters, cut it to the same size as the mats instead, drawing around with a pencil to get the composition right.

3. Using a stiff brush, spread a thin layer of wood glue all over the surface and edge of the mats, then place the magazine pages on top and smooth them down to remove any bubbles. Then, turning the mats over, spread more glue around the edges of the reverse side and wrap the paper carefully around the edges, folding at the corners for a neat shape.

4. To stick cardboard, spread glue onto both the card and the mats or coasters. To prevent curling after sticking, put them to dry between heavy books.

5. Once the glue is dry, trim any excess card with scissors and carefully paint the edges of the mats or coasters with enamel paint – if you're using paper or magazines, the mats don't need this as the paper will wrap right around the edges.

6. The covered mats and coasters now need lots of coats of varnish to stand up to warm plates and cups, spillages and cleaning. As many as ten thin coats are best for a really strong, durable finish, so choose a quick-drying acrylic varnish (water-based, so brushes can be washed in water) to speed up the process.

7. Apply each thin coat of varnish using a good-quality brush to minimise bristle marks. Brush the coats in alternate directions for extra strength and a smoother finish, leaving about an hour between each application.

8. It's also a good idea to varnish the back of each placemat a few times, to make sure the glued edges of the paper are properly sealed.

Spare wallpaper can also be used for this project to create a set of mats that match the décor of your dining room.

Placemats and coasters from rubber flooring
With leftover rubber flooring from a home-improvement project, similar to the covering used for the garden table on page 82, it was easy to make these placemats and coasters for a modern dining room. They are also very easy to look after – they can even be cleaned in the dishwasher.

What you'll need
Leftover rubber flooring material
A straight-edged piece of wood
or a metal ruler
Craft knife
Cutting board

1. This project is so simple, there is only one step! Use the straight edge and craft knife to cut the rubber into the sizes and shapes you want.

Vases and pots made from beer and wine bottles

Like most people, I send hundreds of glass bottles and jars for recycling every year. I thought I'd hold onto a few of them and try this vintage re-use project to make practical vases and pots by breaking them in two.

To cut glass bottles, use a diamond cutter to score the surface of the glass, then apply heat and cold to stress and crack the bottles neatly along the scored line. Or at least that's what's supposed to happen! After consulting many different 'expert' tutorials, and after lots of failed attempts using solvents, string, fire and ice, here's my recommended method for the best chance of making a good clean break, which will only require a small amount of grinding to create a smooth surface afterwards.

1. If you want to remove the labels from your bottles, soak them in soapy water for about an hour and the paper should peel off cleanly. Any stubborn glue residue can be dissolved with white spirit, wiped on with cotton wool.

2. The first step in breaking the bottles is to score a line where you want the crack to form. This creates a flaw in the material, which will concentrate the stresses caused by the heating and cooling process later. You can buy bottle-cutting kits that have a diamond point attached to an arm that fixes to the top of the bottle. These make scoring a neat line (and one that joins up with itself when the bottle is turned through 360 degrees) easier, but such kits can be expensive. Instead, I rigged up a simple homemade frame from a plastic bottle and used an inexpensive diamond glass cutter.

3. To make your cutting frame, cut the top off the plastic bottle then, with a craft knife, cut a small slot in one side, just above the height where you will want to make the lines. This slot is for the tip of the diamond cutter to poke through while a bottle placed inside the plastic is turned around.

4. Support the plastic bottle between heavy books or on a workbench. Secure with tape to make sure it won't turn around. Then, place your wine bottle inside. Add rags or tissues to the closed end of the plastic tube to support the wine bottle and position the slot at the point where you want to score the line.

5. Now, place the diamond cutter through the slot and hold it firmly against the glass. Get your helper to turn the wine bottle very slowly and carefully while you keep the cutter steady at the correct angle to make a scored line. The line should meet up with itself (or be very close) after one whole revolution of the bottle.

6. It's a good idea to score several bottles at a time before moving to the next stage. This process gets much easier with practice, so you will find later attempts are neater.

7. To prepare for breaking the bottles, half fill a sink with water and boil a kettle full of water. Then run a cold tap slowly into the sink.The aim of this stage is to stress the glass gently using alternate hot and cold water to expand and contract the material near the scored line. Eventually, this 'heat stress' will be enough to start a crack, and this should spread along the line all the way around the wine bottle.

Even with this gentler method of applying hot and cold, you will still end up with rejects where the crack has veered away from the scored line due to other defects in the material. So don't try this with anything precious, and be prepared to recycle quite a few failed efforts!

8. The best way of getting a neat line seems to be to apply the heat and cold only in the area of the score. Giving the whole bottle a severe shock (for example by heating it and plunging it into cold water) can trigger cracks to form around other flaws and edges and isn't recommended.

9. Start by holding the bottle by its base, pointing the neck downwards at an angle, and running it under the cold tap for a few seconds. Aim the stream of water at the scored line and turn the bottle so that all sides are cooled evenly.

10. Then, remove the bottle from the flow of water and, holding it at the same angle over the sink, pour a small amount of very hot water from the kettle onto the bottle in the same way, turning it so that all sides are exposed to the heat.

11. After applying hot water for a few seconds, return the bottle to the cold tap, then repeat this process until you hear a tinkling sound or see a crack begin to form within the glass.

12. Once the crack starts to form, continue to apply the hot and cold water treatment, but now concentrate the flow on the areas at each end of the crack. You should be able to see the progress of the crack as it moves around the bottle and, after a while, the top of the bottle will break off and drop into the water below.

13. Repeat this with several bottles, being careful when handling the broken glass, which will be very sharp (don't do this with children nearby!). You should end up with some good candidates for using as vases or containers, and several rejects as well. Dispose of the failures carefully, as well as the broken tops of the successes.

14. The final step is to grind off the sharp edges from the broken bottles and sand down any small flaws. For this, use 'wet and dry' sandpaper. Place a sheet of this paper on a flat surface, add a few drops of water and then rub the bottle over the surface in a circular motion. Taking away the sharpness only takes a few minutes of this treatment. However, if you want to smooth away larger flaws in the edge, you will need more patience. Bottles that haven't broken with a flat edge can be sanded by hand, using a small pieces of folded sandpaper, dipped in water.

3

Restorations
and rebuilds

Restorations and rebuilds

This chapter is about restoring and remaking larger items, and includes some clever ways to change unwanted furnishings, including mending and re-covering a set of shabby dining chairs and converting a broken coat stand into a table.

Some of the projects involve restoring pieces to look as good as new, without fundamentally changing their shape or structure, while others change an item into something completely different with more dramatic changes.

You will need specialist tools for certain projects that you probably don't already have in your toolbox, such as a particular kind of saw or a staple gun. However, if you can't borrow them from a friend, these items aren't expensive to buy and will come in handy for many other tasks in the future. I've used power tools for some of the projects, too, but if you don't have a power sander or jigsaw, you can still get these jobs done – the powered alternative will simply make the job a bit quicker.

Flat-pack furniture also undergoes a transformation. These products are so cheap that it's tempting to chuck them away when they no longer fit perfectly into your home. But, with a bit of imagination, all manner of 'flat-pack hacks' are possible, giving you the exact pieces you need with little or no expense. From an unwanted bookcase I've made a great little sideboard and a very useful media unit for my new home, without spending money on anything more expensive than a bit of wood filler, sandpaper and some paint.

There are lots of ideas for table tops as well, made from items I've bought from reclamation yards or been given by friends and neighbours who have materials left over from their home improvements. Rubber flooring and fireplace tiles are used to make two very different garden tables from a reclaimed iron base. And I've used broken tiles for a small table top on some tubular metal legs.

You can also find out how to undertake easy upholstery with no sewing or complicated techniques, just by adding a piece of new foam and some new fabric with a staple gun. You don't have to copy my projects precisely to be inspired to take on similar revamps in your home. The same techniques, tools and advice can be adapted to many different restoration and rebuilding projects.

A broken coat stand remodelled

This lovely old coat stand was left in pieces on the corner of my street. It had some beautiful, bent wood parts, which I couldn't resist reclaiming. Here I've used second-hand leather clothing, bought from a charity shop, to make two new 'ranch-style' pieces for a hallway.

What you'll need

Coat stand

Spare bits of wood or board to make the table top and the body of the coat rack

Jigsaw or other small saw

Hammer and chisel

Drill

Screws

Leather (or imitation leather) garments from a charity shop – I used a red skirt for this project

Sharp scissors

PVA (wood or craft) glue

Staple gun and staples

1. Remaking the base of a coat stand is simple. The bottom part of the central pole may stick up above the circular rim, however, so be prepared to unscrew this and reattach it to the bent wood feet at a lower level.

2. Once you have a table base, you need to find a suitable piece of sheet material for a table top. I cut a circle from a piece of board with a power jigsaw, but a square top would look just as good.

3. For the coat rack, cut the curved hooks in half, then take a spare block of wood (mine was a chunk from an old door frame) and cut shallow channels to hold the hooks. I used a saw to cut the side walls of the channels and then a chisel to knock out the material between these cuts.

4. Then, drill holes in the hooks so they can be attached within these channels with screws.

5. Now it's time to cover the rack and table top in your leather material. Unpick your garments at the seams and work out the best way to cut and arrange the pieces around the wooden parts.

Covering parts and details with reclaimed leather or PVC is really simple. This idea could be used to wrap many other items, such as small shelves, stools, boxes, frames or the placemats on page 63.

6. Apply a thin layer of wood glue to your table top and wood block. Then, when it is nearly dry, wrap the leather around the pieces and use a staple gun to attach it to the reverse side of each piece. Use lots of staples (they will be out of sight) and pull the leather tight to remove any creases.

7. Finally, construct the finished pieces by attaching the table top to the circular rim and using wood screws to attach the hooks inside the channels at the back of the coat rack.

If the pieces of leather don't quite cover your items, you may need to improvise. The skirt I used wasn't quite long enough to cover my table top, so I used a thin strip to cover the gap in the edge of the table. Then I cut a spare piece of oak-faced board to make a small shelf to cover the gap on top of the table.

Padded chairs transformed

This set of chairs, with their stylish curves, had taken plenty of abuse during years of living with a friend's cat. Starting with battered woodwork and torn covers, here I've given them two different, and equally stylish looks. The new chairs will last for many more years before needing another revamp.

What you'll need

Padded chairs

Pliers

Rubber gloves and protective glasses

Paint stripper

Paint brushes

Wire wool and fine sandpaper

Wood stain, Danish oil and old rags

Foam padding and upholstery wadding

Marker pen

Cutting board

Craft knife and scissors

New covering materials
(I bought durable new materials
for the seats and used vintage fabrics
for the backs and edging)

Staple gun and staples

Spray glue and PVA (wood or craft) glue

Hessian

Fire safety

Old foam and fabrics don't meet modern safety standards so, when re-using old furniture, make sure to add at least one layer of new foam, wadding or fabric that will resist burning. There may be extra rules about re-using soft furnishings in your area, so check for official advice if you are in any doubt about what's permitted.

1. After unscrewing the padded seat and back, the next step is to remove the staples fixing on the existing covers. On my chairs there were hundreds of these, and I used a set of pliers and plenty of effort – doing this in front of the TV helped make it less tedious!

2. The next step is to remove the old varnish from the wood frames. Wearing rubber gloves to protect your skin and glasses to protect your eyes, brush paint stripper onto chair frame, wait 5 minutes for the varnish to blister, then reapply the stripper. Twenty minutes later, the varnish can be scraped off easily.

3. Scrub off any remaining varnish with wire wool, then sand the wood lightly and buff it again with wire wool for a really smooth finish.

4. To darken your wood, apply a suitable wood stain, rubbing it in gently with an old rag. Then, add two applications of Danish oil to help protect the wood. Let each application soak in well before buffing the finished chair frame with a dry rag. This technique gives a durable finish with a gentle sheen that – unlike the varnish – won't chip.

Safety note

Paint stripper can burn your skin or eyes. See page 21 for important notes on using it safely.

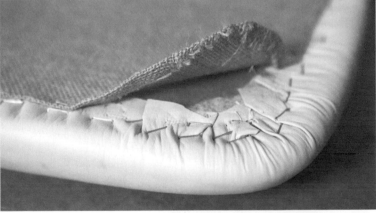

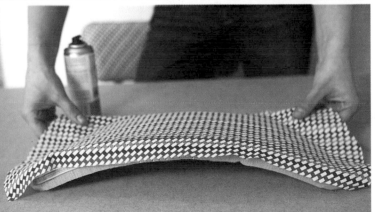

5. You may want to add more padding to the back and seat of your chairs to make them more comfortable. If so, the next step is to measure and cut some extra foam padding. Place the seat and back onto the foam and draw around them with a marker pen to get the correct shape. Then, on a cutting board or spare piece of sheet material, cut out the basic shape with a sharp craft knife (this doesn't have to be done very neatly).

6. Next, tidy up the shape and trim the top corners of the foam with scissors, to soften the edge and create a more rounded shape.

7. Replace the original, thin pads of foam on the base of the seat, then place your new foam on top and wrap up the whole thing in a layer of upholstery wadding, using a few staples on the reverse side of the seat to hold it in place.

8. For the back of my chair, before adding the foam and wadding, I also attached a piece of the new cover fabric to the unpadded rear side, using a thin layer of spray glue to hold it in place (this glue won't soak into the material and discolour it). Then I stapled the wadding around the edge of the wood, rather than wrap it all the way around.

9. The next stage is the most fiddly. To get a smooth, crease-free seat and back, it is important for the final cover material to be stretched very carefully over the foam and wadding, and held in place using plenty of staples. Start by pulling the material very tight over the wadding and adding single staples at the centre points of each side and at each corner. Then, working your way carefully towards each corner, pull, shape, fold and staple the material to make the top surface as smooth as possible, with most of the creases hidden from view on the underside. Sometimes, when reaching a corner, you may find you have excess material or too many folds, which means removing a few staples and repositioning the fabric. Taking this much care is worth it for a neat final result, I promise!

10. For chair seats, the staples will be out of sight beneath the chair, but you can cover these up with a layer of rough hessian to make the whole thing neater. For the seat backs, the lines of staples you will end up with around the edges do need to be hidden. A simple piece of edging fabric glued into place will do the job. I chose a constrasting folded strip cut from the seat fabric for one of my designs, and a strip of matching fabric for the other.

11. Finally, screw the backs and seats onto the wooden frames again.

I had my foam padding cut roughly to size by a local supplier. Foam is very low cost, so don't be afraid to use it to remodel your chair pads if you want extra comfort. You can get upholstery wadding from craft stores or from the same suppliers as the foam and it is also inexpensive.

New table tops for an old iron base

This cast-iron table base was a bargain from a reclamation yard, and its original home was a London pub. I've made two table tops from recycled materials that transform it into very different styles.

For a modern look, I cut a circle from a sheet of spare fibreboard, added a metal strip to give extra depth at the edge (for this strip, I used a long piano hinge), and covered the whole thing in leftover rubber flooring. Then, for a more classic style, I took an old oak door and filled it with early 20th century fireplace tiles (also from the reclamation yard).

Preparing the base

These solid iron table bases suffer only from one problem: rust. This is easy to deal with: simply brush off any loose flakes, then paint the whole thing with a coat of black metallic paint.

Modern table top

1. First measure the piano hinge that you will use to extend the depth of your table for a thick, rubber edge. Calculate the correct size for the circular table top by dividing the length of the hinge by the mathematical constant pi (approximately 3.14). This gives the diameter of the circle you need – in my case this was 57cm.

2. Draw a circle of this size on the fibreboard, cut it out with a jigsaw, then sand off the rough edges. Then, brush on wood preserver to help the board stand up better to damp conditions outside. See the safety note on page 85 for important information about using this chemical safely.

What you'll need

Cast iron table base

Wire brush

Black metallic paint

Paint brushes

A piece of 12mm veneered fibreboard (any spare sheet material would do)

Steel piano hinge or long hinge

Pencil or marker pen

Power jigsaw

Sanding block and sandpaper

Clear wood preserver and paint brush

Solvent-free, 'filler' glue

Small screws and a screwdriver

Rubber flooring

A sharp craft knife

Masking tape

Silicone bathroom sealant

---

3. Then, attach the piano hinge around the edge of the circle of board, using 'filler' glue and a handful of wood screws. (This glue is often sold as being 'as hard as nails' and is a good, cheap hard adhesive for large areas, though it does take up to 24 hours to set properly.)

4. The next step is to cut out a circle of rubber for the top of the table. For this, use a sharp craft knife and the board itself as your guide.

5. Attach the rubber to the board using the same 'filler' glue.

6. Next, cut a number of rubber strips just wider than the hinge (I used a thinner piece of rubber that had been left as a sample when the thicker material was purchased, but you can use the same material as for the top). Glue these strips around the edge of the table, onto the hinge, holding it in place with masking tape wrapped all the way around the circle several times.

7. When the glue has set firmly, sand the bottom of the rubber edging lightly to smooth it off.

8. Finally, to protect the board even better from damp, use clear silicone bathroom sealant on the top edge of the table, smoothing a tiny blob into the gap between the two pieces of rubber with your fingers. To help with a messy job (silicone is very sticky when it comes out of the tube) coat your fingers in liquid soap before starting.

A piano hinge?

It may seem a strange choice to use a long piano hinge, instead of a simpler strip of metal or plastic, to provide an edge for this table. However, I've used piano hinges before to make circular frames and they work well.

Because they are made from two hinged strips, joined at the centre with a rod, they are flexible, but when opened flat and bent into a circle, become very stiff and strong. In addition, they come ready-made with screw holes and are easy to cut to the right length with a hacksaw. Long hinges can be found in most hardware suppliers.

Classic table top

1. Start by cutting the door into a square shape. When you have measured the correct length, cut straight through the whole door, including the frame and the central panel, using a panel saw.

2. This will make a three-sided frame, which your tiles should fit into neatly, but will leave one side incomplete. Rather than try to do complicated woodwork with new tenon joints, I recommend a more improvised approach: simply cut a piece from the inner panel of the remaining piece of door and glue it down to fill the space at one end. Because this will leave a messy looking edge, cut another strip from the leftover frame and nail this over the end to patch it up.

3. You will now have a square table top with a central well to hold the tiles. However, in order for the table to rest safely on the cast-iron base, you will need to reinforce the underside of the central panel. From any spare piece of wood or plywood, cut a piece slightly larger than the central space and nail it to the underside of the table top. Don't worry about doing this neatly either, as it will be out of sight.

4. Next, you will need to protect the wood from rotting in damp conditions. To do this, take the table top outside and apply two coats of clear wood preserver (see the safety note for important information about using this chemical).

5. Now you are ready to place the reclaimed tiles. Started by spreading a thick layer of tile adhesive paste into the table top using a grout spreader (or a homemade version made from cardboard). Then, place the tiles in position and press them down with a long, straight piece of wood to make sure they lie flat and level with the door frame.

What you'll need
Reclaimed interior or exterior door
Measuring tape
Panel saw
PVA (wood or craft) glue
Hammer and nails
A scrap piece of plywood
Clear wood preserver and paint brush
Combined tile adhesive and grout
Grout spreader, or a piece of thick cardboard with serrated 'teeth' cut out
Reclaimed tiles
Sponge scourer and a dry cloth
Large screws and screwdriver

6. After leaving the adhesive to set for 8 hours it will be ready for grouting. Scooping up some of the same combined grout and adhesive compound with the spreader, apply it all over the tiled surface until the spaces between the tiles are filled. Then wipe away excess grout from the surface of the tiles with a wet sponge, using diagonal strokes to avoid pulling the grout from the channels.

7. After the grout has set (another 8 hours), clean and polish the tiles with a soapy sponge scourer and a dry cloth. Then fix the table top securely to the base, using large screws.

Look out for these materials elsewhere in this book – my brick bookcase on page 160 uses shelves made from the oak door panel and the inner wall of the doll's house on page 176 also uses the same wood. More of this rubber flooring material can be seen made into placemats and coasters on page 65.

Safety note

Wood preserver does a great job of protecting wood from damp weather but it must be used very carefully. Before it dries, it is very toxic, volatile and flammable.

Make sure you wear protective gloves, work outdoors in a well ventilated area and work carefully to minimise splashing. Keep the liquid away from food and drink, children, garden ponds, plants and wildlife. And, as an extra precaution, don't let pets near the materials for several days after the preserver has dried. Afterwards, wash everything you've used very carefully, and wash your hands thoroughly before eating or preparing food.

Ideas for tubular metal furniture

No matter how beaten up and shabby it gets, furniture made from tubular metal can almost always be reclaimed and turned into something gorgeous again. All of these projects were made from metal furniture that was thrown away in my neighbourhood.

First, I'll run through the steps for making a peeling plywood and metal chair as good as new. Then, I'll make two very different table tops for reclaimed metal legs: one with broken tiles and one with board game pieces set in resin.

Padded chair

This old plywood chair had been used in a workshop and then left out in the rain, so it was covered in paint and the wood was peeling badly. I repaired the seat back and covered the seat with a new pad and a bright, printed fabric.

1. After removing the seat and backrest from the metal chair frame, sand the frame to remove smears of old paint, then use wire wool to smooth it down further.

2. Before painting the frame, remove any rubber feet and stoppers from the ends of the metal tubes, then apply two or three coats of enamel paint in a suitable colour with a brush.

3. To repair the peeling plywood on the backrest, pull off any layers of wood that are very badly damaged, then push wood glue between the remaining layers and wrap the whole thing tightly in masking tape. Leave overnight to allow the glue to set hard before removing the tape.

What you'll need

Plywood chair
Screwdriver
Sandpaper and coarse wire wool
Enamel paint
Paint brush
White spirit (for cleaning the brush)
PVA (wood or craft) glue
Masking tape
Primer and gloss paint to match the fabric
Small gloss roller and tray
A square of foam
Spray glue
Reclaimed or vintage fabric
Staple gun and staples

4. Sand down any remaining rough surfaces, then prime and paint the backrest with gloss paint, using a foam roller for a professional-looking finish (see page 15 for more guidance on using a roller with gloss paint). Add two or three coats of paint, sanding with fine paper between each coat.

5. Adding a new pad and cover to the seat means you don't have to repair this plywood properly. Simply remove any parts that are peeling away, then cut a piece of foam to the correct size and use spray glue to hold it in place.

6. Ideally the cover material could now be stapled all around the bottom edge of the seat before attaching it to the frame. However, for this frame, the base needed to be screwed on from above, so I stapled just one edge of the fabric, then screwed on the seat before stapling around the other edges with the seat attached to the frame. This took a bit of time to do neatly, but looked good when it was finished.

See the dining chairs project on page 78 for tips on getting a neat, regular finished shape when stapling fabric onto padding furniture.

Table with tiled top

These legs were originally part of a stool. I added a simple tiled top, using offcuts from a neighbour's new bathroom tiles, to make a small side table or plant stand.

1. Spread a dustsheet on the floor. After sanding and scrubbing the legs with wire wool, add two or three coats of enamel paint in your chosen colour.

2. To make the tiled table top, start by cutting a base from any suitable piece of board or wood. Prime and paint this with emulsion paint and let it dry fully before adding the tiles.

3. A good way of making offcuts of tiles look attractive is to break them up into smaller pieces of different sizes (break them with a hammer while covering them with a cloth) so they can be arranged in an irregular pattern.

4. Coloured grout will make plain white tiles look great. You can buy coloured grout or make your own shade by adding a few drops of highly pigmented acrylic paint or powder colour to the grout and mixing well.

5. Fix the tiles to the base by applying a thick layer of combined grout and tile adhesive compound to the base and pressing in the pieces of tile to fit as closely together as possible. Work quickly, then, while the adhesive is still damp, wipe away any excess grout from around the sides of the painted wooden base.

6. Leave the adhesive to dry, then apply the same compound as a grout, pushing it into the gaps between the tiles. Then wipe the surface of the tiles gently to remove smears of excess grout.

When metal tubing isn't part of a welded frame, like these separate leg pieces, painting them can be tricky. I recommend hanging up the pieces so you can reach all the surfaces at once.

7. Once the grout is fully dry (about 8 hours), clean the tiles with a scouring sponge to remove any dried on grout, then polish with a soft cloth.

8. Finally, attach the top to the legs. To make this table stand up securely, I cut a square of hardboard just smaller than the space between the top of the legs and screwed right through the hardboard and the holes in the legs into the bottom of the table top.

Resin table top

One more idea for a small table top is to set small items in clear resin, such as these counters and dice. The tubular legs for this project are from another broken chair I found in the street that I painted with enamel paint using the same technique as for the tiled table and chair. I bought the tiny dice new and used two sets of counters from second-hand games to fill a wooden frame that I found in a charity shop.

What you'll need

A shallow frame to hold the resin –
this can be wood, metal or any material
that can be painted

Gloss paint in a suitable background colour

Clear silicone sealant and applicator

Counters or beads

Spirit level

Pieces of card

Two-part clear polyurethane resin
(kits can be bought from craft stores and
internet suppliers)

Duct tape or glue

1. Prepare the frame by painting with a solvent-based gloss paint.

2. It's important that the resin mixture doesn't leak out so, next, seal the edges and corners with clear silicone sealant. Using an applicator, pipe a thin bead along the corners, then wipe along with a wet finger covered in detergent to smooth it off.

3. Use small blobs of the same silicone sealant to stick the counters inside the frame. This will ensure they stay exactly in the arrangement you want when you pour in the resin. Allow the sealant to dry for at least 24 hours before moving on to the next stage.

4. Before mixing and pouring the resin, heat your frame gently. This will help the resin to flow easily into all the gaps between the counters. About 50ºC is enough – use an electric oven on a very low heat, or pop the frame on top of a hot radiator for an hour.

5. Put your frame on a level surface for pouring. Make sure it is perfectly flat, using a spirit level and pieces of card pushed under the corners.

6. Mix the resin using the precise instructions that come with your kit. For two-part liquid resins, you need to mix together the two parts carefully, trying to avoid adding air bubbles as you stir them together. You will have about 10 minutes to complete the pouring process, before the mixture starts to thicken and set.

7. Pour the resin mixture slowly into the frame. Fill it about halfway, then tap sharply on the side of the frame a few times to release air from around and under the counters. Then add the rest of the resin until all the counters are covered completely. Tap on all the sides again, to release even more bubbles (unless you use a vacuum chamber, you'll always have to live with some bubbles appearing in the resin, but these won't ruin the final effect).

8. While the resin sets, be careful not to allow dust, hair and other dirt to fall onto its surface.

9. After the resin has completely hardened, all you have to do is attach the frame to a base. You can't screw into the resin from below, so use duct tape or glue to secure the frame.

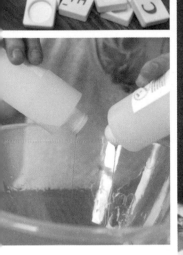

You can set a wide range of small items in resin using this technique. While the resin sets, it generates heat and any dampness will also cause bubbles to form. So, avoid using natural, living materials (such as leaves) for this project.

Before buying resin, calculate carefully the volume of space you will need to fill, remembering to deduct the volume of the items you will be placing inside. School maths comes in useful for making these estimates! A variety of resin compounds can be purchased from craft suppliers. Polyurethane is heat-resistant and transparent, which makes it a good choice for this project.

Flat-pack hacks

Inexpensive flat-pack furniture is surprisingly easy to re-model into new pieces. It tends to be made economically from composite materials that are simple to cut and reshape, and parts are normally fixed together with removable 'knock-down' joints, so they can be dismantled and put back together in new ways.

What you'll need

Tall bookcase

Panel saw

Drill

Screwdriver and screws

Wood filler

Corrugated cardboard scraps

Sandpaper (various grades) and sanding block (or an electric palm sander to save time)

Wood primer

Paint brush

Gloss paint in two colours

Small gloss roller and tray

Thick cardboard tube

Masking tape

Scissors

Wallpaper

Wallpaper paste

Add a new colour scheme and, for very little money and a small amount of effort, you can have unique, bespoke furniture tailored to your own tastes. Here I'll show two ideas for remodelling flat-pack items you can find in almost every home: lightweight lacquered coffee tables and tall bookcases.

A bookcase turned into a sideboard and media unit
When I moved into a house with a cellar, this tall bookcase, which had been used for filing, wasn't needed, but I did have space for more furniture in the living and dining rooms. So, I turned the bookcase into two new pieces of furniture by cutting it in half. The top part is now a pretty sideboard and the bottom part became a neat unit for storing electronics.

Sideboard
Turned on its side, with a coat of paint, the top half of my bookcase is now a sideboard. The only challenge was giving it suitable feet. This was resolved when I found a thick cardboard tube outside my local dry cleaners.

1. Before starting, take the hardboard backing sheet off the bookcase. This will be held on with small tacks and easy to remove with pliers or just by pulling it away gently.

2. Most flat-pack bookcases will have one fixed shelf near the centre of the unit, while the other shelves will be held up with small pegs, placed in rows of holes in each side. The best place to cut a similar bookcase in half for these projects is just above the fixed shelf. This will provide a solid top for the media unit and a sideboard with a good length.

Spare wallpaper can be used to brighten up flat-pack bookcases and units even if you don't remodel them. Use leftovers from decorating a wall or use a sample piece from the same range in a contrasting colour scheme.

Use a large panel saw to slice straight through the unit – it will be very easy to cut, as the centre of the boards making up the sides are likely to be filled with lightweight chipboard or (in this case) thin cardboard.

3. To add a new side wall, and to give the unit strength, fix one of the spare shelves between the cut ends. Drill small holes through the sides, close to the front and back of the unit where the boards will have solid edges. Then drill some shorter, larger countersink holes (so the screws can sit below the surface) and use long wood screws to fix the shelf in place.

4. Next, you will need to fill and reshape the cut end of the sideboard. You can do this with wood filler but, if large holes need to be filled, work in several stages, letting each application dry before adding more filler. For very large holes, plug them first with scraps of corrugated card. At the final stage, apply excess filler over the whole area and slightly around each edge. Then, sand carefully to get a really clean and neat finished shape.

5. Now the basic construction has been completed, it's time to work on the surfaces. The original bookcase is likely to be lacquered or sealed with plastic so, to get a painted finish that won't easily scratch or peel, you need to roughen up this surface before priming and painting. Go over the whole unit with rough 'paint stripping grade' sandpaper until every part is thoroughly scratched and dull.

6. Next add two coats of primer. Brush on a thick layer (applying extra to any cut surfaces, and to the wood filler) then sand with medium paper before adding a further, thinner coat. Sand again before starting the painting process, to remove brush marks.

7. A really smooth finish can be achieved with gloss paint and a small foam roller (see page 15 for more tips on this technique). Use three or four coats, sanding with fine sand paper after each one has dried.

8. Next, think about the internal shelves you will want in your unit. In my example, I've re-used the original shelves and fixings to make two vertical walls and fixed a third, horizontal, shelf onto these. To support the metal pegs for this third shelf, I drilled small holes in the vertical shelves.

9. Sand, prime and paint the shelves in the same way as the rest of the unit, using contrasting colours if this works with your design.

10. A sideboard also needs feet to support it away from the floor. This can be a great opportunity to re-use parts of other furnishings or improvise like me by cutting a thick cardboard tube into quarters. Paint your feet to match the sideboard or use a complementary colour. I've also added a strip of white to the bottom of my feet, using masking tape to get a good line.

11. Finally, replace the back-board, having first cut it to size and covered it with wallpaper before reattaching with tacks.

Media unit
The bottom part of my bookcase had a fixed shelf at the top and the original feet, so it didn't need a lot of reconstruction work.

1. After cutting away the top part of the bookcase, fill and reshape the cut ends of the side panels. Use wood filler, along with cardboard to plug any large holes in the same way as you did for the end of the sideboard.

2. When the wood filler has dried and has been sanded smooth, follow the same process of priming and painting the sideboard (steps 6–7) to give your unit a strong, durable finish.

3. Do the same with any shelves you want to use for your electronic equipment or simply keep the original wood-effect, as I have done here.

4. Once you know where your shelf will be placed, cut a hole in the backing sheet at the correct height to allow wires for your electronic equipment to pass neatly out of the back of the unit.

Coffee table stack

Boxy flat-pack coffee tables are ideal for fixing together in different arrangements to make a custom, multi-level unit.

I've added primary colours and created a modern abstract design, but you could use any colours that fit your home, or why not try découpage on some of the parts for a prettier look?

What you'll need

Flat-pack coffee tables
Measuring tape
Paper and pencil
Panel saw
Medium sandpaper and sanding block
Corrugated cardboard
Wood filler
Strips of hardboard
PVA (wood or craft) glue
Primer, paint and paintbrushes
Drill
Corner brackets
Screws, long bolts and nuts

Use 'knock-down' joints with screws and bolts, rather than gluing your unit together. This is stronger and also makes it easy to take the unit to pieces if it needs to be moved.

1. First, measure the coffee tables, then sketch out a new design and carefully calculate the sizes of the different surfaces and legs you will need.

2. Next, cut all the pieces to the correct sizes using a panel saw. Sand the cut ends smooth with a medium grade sandpaper.

3. Because the legs for these tables attach to the table tops with long screws, you will need to fill in any hollow areas where the legs will be attached in places that were not the original corners.

To do this, cut strips of corrugated cardboard to the same height as the hollow spaces, spread a layer of wood filler over the card and roll it up before pushing it into the new corners. Spread more wood filler into any gaps and leave it all to dry. This will leave a good, solid chunk of material to screw into later.

4. Now create new side panels for any parts of the table tops that will be exposed when the unit is finished. You may find that you can re-use the sides of pieces you have cut away or you can cut strips of hardboard and use these instead.

5. Glue the new sides in place, then fill in any gaps with wood filler before sanding smooth.

6. Now you are ready to paint or cover the different parts. I've used gloss paint in a range of colours, sanding the lacquered surface first and using primer followed by several coats of paint. Follow the steps for painting the sideboard on page 96 to get a good finish with gloss paint.

7. Now that all the pieces of your unit are ready, drill pilot holes for screws in any new corners and attach the legs to each table. Then, you can plan for fixing the different parts together to make your unit. Small corner brackets are ideal for this. Because the legs are hollow, placing the brackets so they fit inside the legs means that you only need to add a small screw on the outside. You can paint over this later to make it virtually invisible. Be careful to choose the placement of these brackets to ensure that these screws end up at the back of the legs.

8. At the corners of the surfaces, where the material is solid, you can simply screw the brackets into the top surfaces. In places where the material is hollow, a stronger method is to put a long bolt through a hole drilled right through the table top, fixing it with a nut.

Junk Fiends: Hilary Bruffell

Hilary Bruffell's Moroccan-style day-beds are an inspired idea for re-using indoor furniture to provide comfort and style outside in the garden.

'I started with a horrible old pine double bed that was surplus to requirements, removed the bottom end and cut it in half to make arms, then sliced through the base to create something the shape of a long seat.

'Then I treated the whole thing with exterior wood preserver. The thing about the softwood used for interiors is that it can rot, so protecting it from the weather is important. I reapply the preservative every year and cover it up in the winter, since it's too big to bring inside. Placing slate roof tiles under the feet also helps to keep the wood out of harm's way when it rains.

> **'It will last for many years, but I will be keeping a close eye on the condition of the seat planks, just in case they ever need replacing.'**

Hilary's style is influenced by trips to Marrakech, so she has mixed together different coloured and patterned fabrics to cover the cushions, some of which were also salvaged from an old sofa. 'I trawl second-hand shops and warehouse sales for anything bright that catches my eye. I'm a real magpie!' she says.

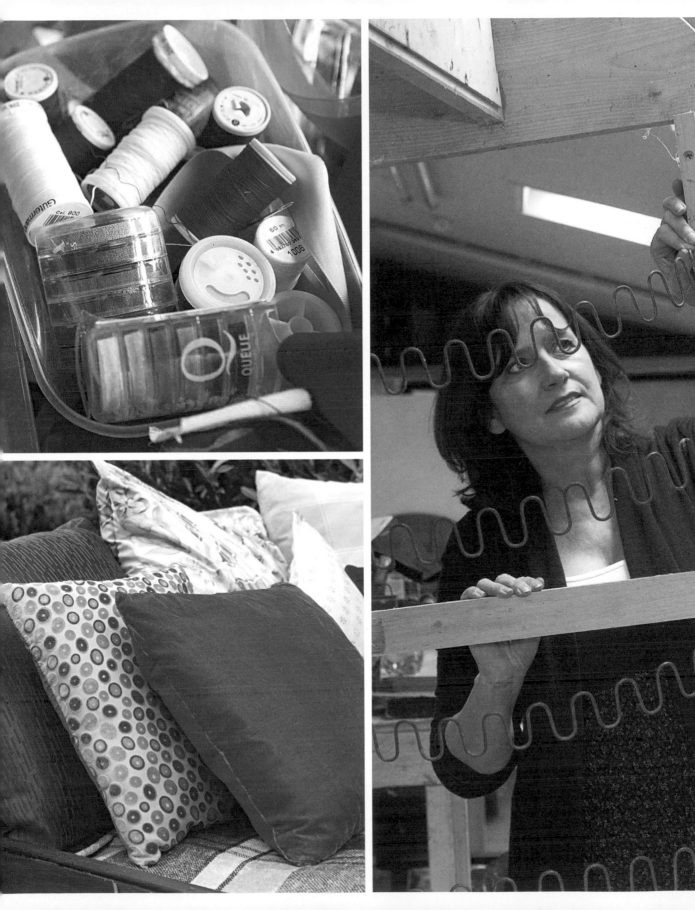

The result, placed under a pergola in a corner that catches the evening sun, is the perfect haven to relax in the garden at the end of a long day. Hilary calls it 'my gin-and-tonic place, and it's a lovely spot to sit and chat with a friend.'

The day-bed has proved such a success that Hilary has repeated the idea at her second home in Spain and has made another seat for her English garden from her son's old single bed. Despite the weather-proofing stain, the graffiti written in marker pen when he was a child still shows through, providing a timeless reminder of its previous life.

Hilary certainly needs a place to wind down. As well as working as a research psychologist, she's a founder member of the 'Make It And Mend It' website and blog, which promotes re-use and creative crafts. The team behind MIAMI – Clare Flynn, Clare O'Brien, Anne Caborn and Hilary – got together in 2008 after meeting at a conference as part of their day jobs. During a coffee break, the four women realised they all shared a passion for making and mending things and decided to set up the website straight away.

Each brings a different talent to the team. 'Anne knows everything about DIY and loves her drills. Clare O'Brien is a fantastic cook, while Clare Flynn knows everything about the joys of gardening. I'm the real maker of the bunch,' says Hilary.

As a psychologist, she also understands the boost to well-being that comes from making and mending things. 'It just makes you feel good, and the key to that is what we call "self-efficacy" – knowing you have some control of how a job will turn out, and the feeling of achievement when you've finished.'

'I run courses in basic sewing, cushion-making and refashioning clothes, as well as Christmas craft workshops. What I notice is how relaxed people get when they are working together. We have a great time at the workshops and will chat about quite personal things, despite only knowing people for a few hours.'

So, what's next for Hilary and MIAMI? 'The interest in the website just grows and grows, and we're aiming to do more practical things face-to-face in the future. Making and mending is part of the zeitgeist now, and it's not just about people wanting to save money. It's a growing interest in "creative sustainability" where we want more things we can keep for a lifetime, rather than constantly throwing stuff away.

'I've also got a long list of projects to finish at home. I'm hoping to bring another sofa outside and remake it so that plants will actually grow through the structure – that's going to be a very interesting challenge!'

Fabulous fabrics

FABULOUS FABRICS

Junk shops and attics may be full of old fabrics in very bright, bold patterns that look great when used for cushions and accessories. Such fabric finds are either completely free (if they are lying around your house already) or cheap to buy. Here, I'll show you how to bring these materials back into use with a set of projects that focus on upcycling old fabrics into fabulous items for your home.

In this chapter, out-of-date neckties, old jeans and curtains are turned into cushion covers, vintage fabrics are used to cover and co-ordinate smaller household items, and kimonos are recycled into a cushion and a cover for a padded dressing stool.

You can complete all these projects sewing by hand if you don't have a sewing machine. None of the techniques I've used is any more complicated than sewing a straight seam and, for these, the only stitches you need to know are the easy 'running stitch' and, where a stronger seam is needed, a simple 'back-stitch'.

Smaller scraps of material are also recycled into creative projects, used both outside and inside fabric items. A rag rug can absorb almost any kind of fabric into a pattern and small squares and off-cuts are used to cover and stuff a sausage-dog draught excluder.

PATCHWORK CUSHION COVERS

There's almost no limit to the creativity you can employ in making these patchwork cushions. A sewing machine speeds up the process, but you can also complete these projects sewing by hand. If so, you might want to use bigger sections of fabric to reduce the number of seams. However, since this project can be done in front of the fire or the TV, you can complete a more complex pattern over several evenings and it still won't feel like hard work!

What you'll need

Fabric strips and squares

Good sharp scissors

Pins

Needle and thread or sewing machine

Iron for pressing ties and seams

Zips in suitable colours

Cardboard star template

Sourcing materials

A very wide range of recycled and reclaimed materials can be used for cushions. Some are not suitable for machine-washing (such as kimono silk) and cushions made from these fabrics should be used in areas where there's a low risk of getting dirty, to avoid repeated dry cleaning. In the examples shown here I've tried out the following ideas:

* Denim from old jeans in different shades, to make a 'stars and stripes' patterned pillow.

* A range of bright turquoise fabrics, including a large curtain found in a charity shop, a thick, vintage dressmaking material and some off-cuts of turquoise crêpe from a department store.

* A pink and orange patchwork to match the re-covered dressing stool (shown on page 107). This combines vintage silk kimono material with a swatch of an American 1930s print and a blue 1970s flower pattern.

* A diagonal patchwork of unpicked and pressed ties. For business wear, most of these polyester patterns went out of style a long time ago but look great made into cushions for a den or study when used in contrasting stripes. Getting the creases out of the unpicked tie material can be tough, but a few minutes of determined pressing using a steam iron will usually do the job.

Let your imagination run wild: almost any kind of fabric can be used to make patchwork cushion covers.

1. The basic process for constructing any of these cushions is the same. If, like me, you are a lazy seamstress, one of the great things about these projects is that only one side of the finished work matters, so you can get away with all kinds of improvisation and untidiness on the inside!

2. Create squares or rectangles for each side of the cushion separately, pinning the pieces of the pattern together two at a time, then sewing with the machine or by hand. Flatten the seams by spreading them out on the reverse side and pressing with an iron.

3. Place the finished sides facing inwards to each other, then pin and sew around three sides of each cushion, leaving one side free for a zip. These seams don't need to be pressed.

4. I prefer to sew my zips by hand, using a stronger back-stitch, because this is the area where the cushion covers will get most punishment. I also find it easier to make final adjustments to the shape when sewing by hand than when a seam is zooming through the machine.

5. Starting with the zip closed and the cover now turned the right way out, first pin the zip onto one of the good sides and add a folded strip of spare material to act as 'piping' between the zip and the cover. Place the zip so that the pull-tab will be on the outside of the finished cover. The piping should be a few centimetres longer than the edge, so that the spare ends can be tucked neatly inside the corners of the finished cushion.

6. The final step is to line up the other side of the cushion cover and use a couple of pins to mark where the zip needs to go. Then, open up the zip and pin the other side in place (with another strip of piping) before sewing up. Any untidiness around the corners can then be fixed with a few stitches on the inside of the cover.

Decorations
To make decorative stars for the denim pillow, I cut out slightly larger shapes using a cardboard template, then folded and sewed the edges with contrasting hems, by hand. To save time, I used iron-on webbing to attach them to the cover, but decorations and patches like these can be sewn into place almost as easily.

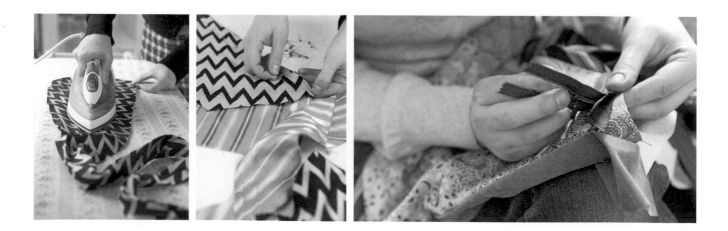

COVER A DRESSING TABLE STOOL

This padded dressing table stool was used for many year by my grandmother, and now belongs to my sister. Its removable furry cover had been washed too many times and was looking old and tired, so I was given the challenge of making some new covers.

I came up with two totally different ideas. The first uses reclaimed French floral cotton fabric, while the second uses bright, stretchy vintage kimono silk.

Repaint the legs

The paint on the legs of the stool was yellowing, so I sanded the surfaces gently and repainted them. I used the same shade of radiator paint as the filing cabinet project on page 150. The soft lilac colour complements both the floral pattern and the bright kimono silk, so the two elasticated covers are interchangeable.

Cover the old foam with wadding

Because this project re-uses old foam padding and vintage fabric, it's important to do something to improve the fireproofing of this project. You could replace the foam padding or use new fabric for a covering, or do what I have here and add a layer of new upholstery wadding over the foam.

Cut the wadding to size then wrap it around the stool and staple underneath before measuring and sewing the covers.

See the notes on page 78 for important additional points on fire safety and fabric furnishings.

What you'll need

Reclaimed cotton fabric

Measuring tape

Scissors

Sewing machine or needle and thread

Iron

Pins

Matching bias tape

Piping cord

Thick elastic

Safety pin or small button

Vintage cotton cover

1. Start by measuring and cutting the pieces of fabric. You'll need one piece to fit the top surface of the foam and further strips to go all around the edges. Allow 2cm for a seam allowance and some extra depth around the sides, so you can sew a channel for elastic.

2. Sew the side strips together to make one continuous loop of fabric that fits closely around the stool. Press the seams flat.

3. The next stage is to add the top seams, including piping. To get a good fit, this is best done on the stool itself. Lay the top piece on the foam with the 'wrong' side facing up. Similarly, take the loop of fabric for the sides and fit this, inside out, around the stool. Arrange it so that the seams in the sides are in unobtrusive places.

4. Prepare a piece of piping long enough to go all the way around the top edge of the stool by wrapping bias tape around a length of piping cord.

5. Now you can pin together your seams. Starting in the middle of one edge, place the piping between the top and side pieces and pin through all the pieces close to the cord. Pin all the straight edges, leaving 2–3 cm of each seam free at each corner. Make sure that the unpinned piping is long enough to go right around each corner, without kinks.

6. Remove the pinned cover from the stool and sew the straight edges by hand or with a machine, leaving the corners free. Remove all the pins.

7. Now replace the cover (still with the right side facing inwards) on the stool. It's best to sew the piping into the corners by hand, with the cover in place on the stool. This helps to get a neat curve.

8. When the corners are finished, add a hem at the bottom for the elastic to go through. Again, measure and pin this with the cover in place, inside out. Then, remove from the stool and sew all the way around, leaving a 1cm gap at one corner. Attach a safety pin or small button to the elastic before pulling it all the way through the channel. Don't tie up the ends yet.

9. The final step is to turn the cover the right way round, fit it to the stool and then tie the elastic at a tension that will hold the cover in place neatly, without bunching up the fabric.

What you'll need

Reclaimed stretchy fabric

Measuring tape

Scissors

Sewing machine or needle and thread

Pins

Thick elastic

Safety pin or small button

Reclaimed kimono silk cover

This stretchy fabric doesn't need piping, so this was a much quicker project than the cotton cover. Reclaimed kimono silk is available from online stockists, or you could complete the same project using any similar fabric item with a bit of stretch, such as a vintage dressing gown.

1. Start by measuring and cutting the fabric. Allowing about 1cm at each edge, cut one piece to fit the top surface and strips for each of the edges. Allow extra depth for the sides, so you can sew a channel for the elastic to go through.

2. Sew the side strips together to make one continuous loop of fabric that fits around the stool snugly. There's no need to press the seams.

3. Next, pin everything together. Doing this 'in situ' is even more important with a stretch fabric, where you want the cover to fit closely (but not too tightly) when slightly stretched. Lay the top piece on the foam with the 'wrong' side facing up and fit the loop of fabric inside-out around the sides. Make sure the seams in the sides end up in appropriate places.

4. Pin together the seams with the cover on the stool, then remove and sew the straight edges, leaving about 2–3cm free at each corner.

5. Replace the cover on the stool, keeping it inside out, and sew up the corners, pulling everything neatly together so there are no folds.

6. Next, measure and pin a hem around the bottom edge for the elastic to pass through. Remove the cover from the stool, and sew this up, leaving a gap of about 1cm at one of the corners.

7. Finally, add your elastic, using a safety pin or button to pull it all the way through the channel. Turn the cover the right way round and place it on the stool before tying off the ends of the elastic at the correct tension.

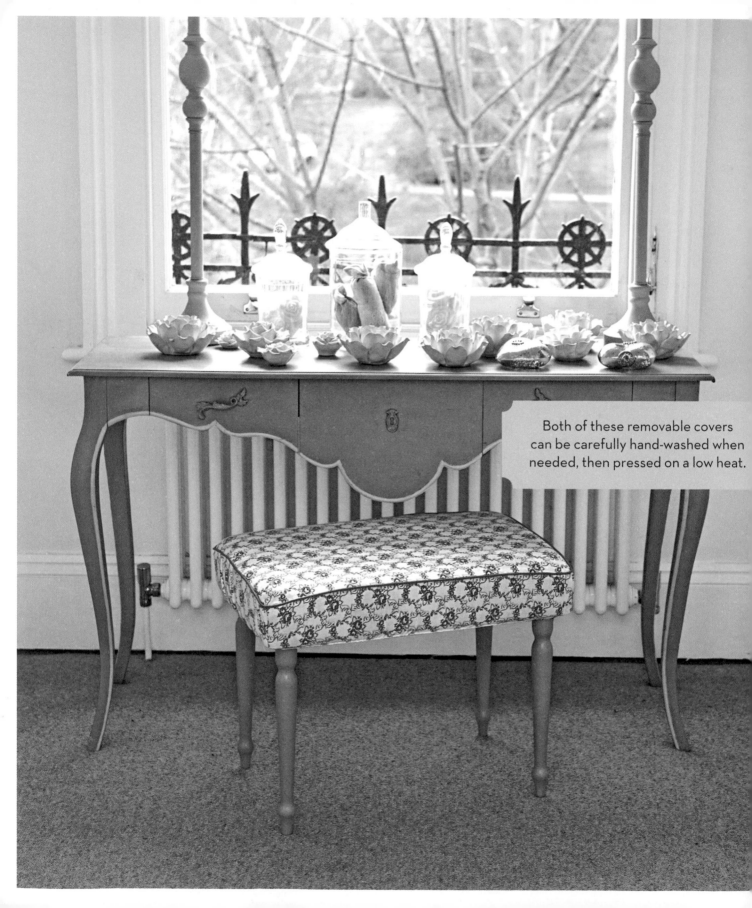

Both of these removable covers can be carefully hand-washed when needed, then pressed on a low heat.

A RAG RUG MADE FROM FABRIC SCRAPS

A rag rug is a real labour of love. Making one of any size is definitely not a 'quick and easy' project; it can take many weeks – if not months – of evenings spent hooking and sewing to complete.

However, like many crafts, it's a very therapeutic pastime and ideal for doing in short bursts of activity, especially if most of these take place on the sofa after dinner. And when you have finished the sense of satisfaction is hard to beat!

It's also a brilliant way to recycle scraps of fabric. For the method I've chosen, the strips of material are very small so can come from many different sources. Cut-offs from other projects, worn out clothing, remnants from shops, T-shirts, socks, out-of-fashion skirts and tops, ribbons, linings and curtains have all gone into my multicoloured rag rug.

Which technique to use?

There are almost as many options as there are rugs. Some rag rugs are made by plaiting fabrics together then coiling up the plaits and sewing them together, but most techniques involve pulling or pushing fabric strips through a base sheet of coarse hessian. Some methods use long strips of fabric, pulled through along their length in a series of loops, but this reduces the potential for using up smaller scraps that might be too short. Others tie the fabric to the hessian by pulling the fabric through itself (similar to the knots in woollen carpets). I found this method also limited the choice of scraps, because thicker fabrics were impossible to pull through the knots.

Another technique simply involves using a hook to pull folded loops of fabric part-way through the hessian and relies entirely on the pressure of the fabric to stay in place. This is a quick technique, and a great way to make a wall hanging, but thinner fabrics can easily pull out, so it isn't a very secure way to make a long-lasting floor rug.

After trying out several options, my favourite technique combines a simple hooking technique with sewing off at the back. This method makes a durable rug and can also incorporate fabric scraps of almost any weight or size.

What you'll need

Fabric scraps

Squared paper

Pencil

A piece of coarse hessian about 15cm larger than the size of your rug

Permanent marker pens

Sharp scissors

Tape measure or ruler

A large needle

Thick cotton cord

A small latch hook (available from craft stores)

---

1. Start by planning your design. Using scraps means that you can't complete large blocks in a completely even colour. However, if you put the fabrics you have available together in similar 'colour groups', it should be relatively easy to devise a two- or three-colour design that uses a blend of different coloured scraps for each shade.

2. Sketch the design on squared paper and decide on the dimensions before drawing the design onto your hessian using permanent marker pens (these lines will be hidden when the rug is complete, but it's important they don't fade until you are finished). You'll be working from the back of the rug, so remember to reverse the design when marking it up.

3. Now cut out enough fabric scraps for the first chunk of the design. This technique uses approximately one scrap for every square centimetre of the design. Each piece needs to be 8–9cm long and 2cm wide.

4. Ensure you mix up pieces from all the materials that make up a 'colour group' when making each batch of scraps. It's not a good idea to use larger pieces of material in sequence, as this will cause abrupt changes in shade.

5. Now you're ready to start hooking. Start by threading the needle with a long piece of cotton cord and tying this onto the hessian at the corner of the design. The cord will be used to secure the loops at the back of the hessian after you pull each one through.

6. To make a loop, put the end of the hook through the hessian from the reverse side. Push the hook through until the hinged latch comes out on the front side. Then, holding a strip of fabric by its ends, grab the centre of the strip with the hook, flip the latch so that the hook encloses the fabric loop, then pull the loop gently through to the reverse side until about 1cm is showing.

7. To help secure the loop on the reverse side, use the needle to sew the cotton cord through the centre of the loop twice.

8. Add the next loop about 1cm from the first and thread the cord through the back of this loop as well, so that the two loops are sewn together. This is what helps build up a strong rug with the rags securely held in place.

9. Continue adding strips of fabric in this way to build up the pattern. Work in rows or squares out from the corner, changing to rags of a different colour group when you reach the marked lines. Don't be tempted to try to complete all the areas of one colour and then fill in between them. Because you need to reach round to the front to add each strip to the hook, you always want to be moving into areas of unworked hessian rather than constantly lifting up a (very heavy) part-completed rug.

10. When you have completed the design, you need to finish off the edges and (if you wish) add an additional layer of hessian to cover the back. Trim off any frayed hessian before folding it under to the back of the rug. Sew around the edge, then cut a further piece of hessian slightly larger than the finished rug, fold its edges in and sew this on, over the loops.

Care tips

As with most rugs and carpets, simple vacuuming should be enough to keep it in good order. If a spillage occurs that needs cleaning, the secure fixing at the back should mean it is safe to wash and tumble dry without falling apart (if the rug is too big for your machine, use the special 'duvet' machines at a local launderette).

Some of the fabrics may not be strictly 'suitable for washing', but if some of the scraps shrink, the overall look of the rug should stay the same.

If you've used a lot of woollen fabrics, your rug might be attractive to clothes moths. If so, you can ward them off without using harsh chemicals by placing the rug inside a freezer for 24 hours (folded up in a plastic bag) once every few months.

Junk Fiends: Gabrielle Treanor

Gabrielle Treanor makes gorgeous garlands. From recycled paper hearts to varying shades of chequered blue fabric, each string has colours, shapes and textures to perk up any home, and now she's turning her talents into a successful business.

'People automatically think of garlands as something in the garden for a party. Personally, I think they can work in any room, and a lot of people use my products in children's bedrooms. They are really gaining popularity as a permanent decoration.' Gabrielle's garlands are mostly made from recycled scraps and off-cuts. 'The idea is so versatile, you can make them out of pretty much anything you can find.

'As a child I would love the colours and textures of the fabrics in my mum's sewing box. One day, she was having a clear out and I seized on all the lovely old 1970s prints to make little flags. Eventually, I needed more fabrics but I couldn't really afford to buy any. That's when I started to look at clothing in charity shops and thinking, "Well, that shirt isn't something I'd want to wear, but the fabric is lovely. Can I use it?" It's all evolved from the need to be thrifty and not spend a lot of money on new fabrics.

'Making a garland doesn't need any special skills, and is so quick when you use a machine to sew them together. When I started, it was a bit of a struggle to remember my sewing lessons at school but the basics came back, like riding a bicycle.

'Cutting out and making is a very calm and satisfying activity. When I work in my other job – as a writer for a children's newspaper – there is satisfaction in seeing the words on a page, but having something physical to hold at the end of a project is a better, more permanent feeling.'

One of the most striking things about Gabrielle's creations is the way she combines different colours. 'I love experimenting with different palettes. With my friend Kirsty, who is also a designer, I play a game called 'palette ping-pong' where we challenge each other to find combinations of colours that work together – or that clash, but in interesting ways. That experimentation has helped to hone my eye and led to some great products in my shop, such as flags in combinations of turquoise and brown.'

> **'That's when I started to look at clothing in charity shops and thinking, "Well, that shirt isn't something I'd want to wear, but the fabric is lovely. Can I use it?"'**

Gabrielle's range of projects soon expanded. Inspired by a shirt she was cutting into scraps, she started remaking whole items. 'My brainwave was realising that a buttoned shirt front would make the perfect opening for a cushion. I tried a few patterns then came up with a way to make an entire cushion out of a shirt. I've made an online tutorial video and used the idea for some great gifts. Recently, I made a christening present for a friend's little boy from one of his dad's old shirts.

'A 'remade' service is now a big part of what I do. For example, if a little girl has grown out of a special dress, her parents might commission me to turn it into a cushion or bag so they can still use it and look at it. I'm a bit sentimental, but it's such a nice feeling to make something like that.'

Honing her skills for business is Gabrielle's current project, and she has now set up her own online store. 'It's going well because there's a growing market for things that are made by hand. My products have been featured in glossy magazines and I get plenty of sales through personal recommendations. More people are thinking about where their stuff comes from and identify with my values of reducing waste. The great thing is that they are prepared to spend a little more as well, recognising that hand-made items take longer to produce than something off a production line.

'Despite difficult economic times, more businesses like mine are springing up everywhere – often created by women looking for new or more rewarding careers. These "kitchen table businesses" fill a niche that is good for the environment and for family life too, so I hope it will continue to grow.'

As well as making things for sale, Gabrielle also fills her blog with printable designs that she gives away. 'People out there are really generous. When I first started out, there were so many resources, and so much help being given away on the internet, that I wanted to give something back too.'

One of the most popular downloads is a poster designed with a quote from the book *Anne of Green Gables*. 'It's my favourite book of all time, and the reason my business is called The Green Gables. The poster says "One can dream so much better in a room where there are pretty things," and that really sums up how I feel about what I do.'

CO-ORDINATED CONTAINERS

Fabric isn't just for soft furnishings. Covering furniture and accessories in matching colours and patterns is quick and easy, and an excellent way to bring together a new look for a room.

You can cover almost anything, as long as its surface isn't heavily textured or irregular. These metal wastepaper bins were ideal for turning into a matching bin and plant holder.

What you'll need

Wastepaper bins or any similar
containers with flat surfaces

Fabric – light-or medium-
weight fabrics work best

Measuring tape or ruler

Pencil

Sharp scissors

Newspaper or dust sheet

Brick

Masking tape

Spray glue

Clear glue

1. Clean and dry your container.

2. Measure and cut a piece of fabric so that it slightly overlaps around the circumference and also at the top and bottom. Make sure the cut edge that will lie on the outside of the overlap is very straight and neat.

3. Cover a table in lots of newspaper or a dust sheet, then put a brick on top and place your container on top of the brick. Raising an item up above the surface like this enables you to apply the fabric neatly when it's longer than the height of the container.

4. Protect any parts that you don't want to get sticky with masking tape (for example, the metal rim of one of my bins).

5. Spray a thick layer of glue all over the outside of the container.

6. Wrap the fabric around the outside, press down from the centre and smooth around the container towards the point where the two edges will meet.

7. Make sure the overlapping seam is straight (if you need to adjust the fabric, you will be able to peel it off and re-attach it for a short time before the glue sticks firm). Leave the glue to dry.

8. Now you need to stick the edges of the fabric to the bottom and inside of your container. Apply a layer of clear glue to the inside edge and around the base and let it dry slightly, so that it is tacky rather than liquid.

> See the filing cabinet project on page 150 for another idea – covering drawer fronts in reclaimed kimono fabric.

9. Then, fold down the fabric, which should stick instantly to the glued surfaces when pressed down. Around the base, let any excess fabric stand up in folds, then snip these off with the scissors. This is better than leaving the folds in place, which could make the base uneven.

10. To finish off, seal the cut edges of the fabric where it lies against the surface of the container by applying a thin bead of glue and wiping it down with a wet finger. This will help stop the edges from fraying.

DOGGY DRAUGHT EXCLUDER

My cute sausage dog helps stop winter draughts coming into my home from the hallway; it was made and stuffed with fabrics left over from the other projects in this chapter.

The floral fabrics came from the dressing table stool on page 111, and the grey faux-suede was used as backing for the tie cushions on page 108. Your draught excluder will look equally cute if he's made from a more random patchwork of colours. Making a three-dimensional stuffed shape like this isn't as hard as it looks. The pieces that make up the basic parts of the head are easy to adapt to create different shapes. When you add their eyes and nose, almost any design will spring to life with its own unique character.

What you'll need
Paper and pencil

Tape measure

Scissors

Scraps and strips of spare or recycled fabrics

A bag full of smaller scraps of wool, wadding, foam, or any material suitable for use as stuffing

Sewing machine or needle and thread

Pins

Button-type teddy bear eyes and nose, with secure washer fixings

Upholstery wadding

1. Start by sketching out your design. Planning the body of your dog is simple and doesn't need a pattern – just measure the bottom edge of your door and work out how long the main 'sausage' needs to be. Then decide how thick you want the body and multiply by about three to get the width of fabric needed.

2. Next draw pieces in the shape of a foot, a tail, the side of a dog's head and an ear. Make these about 30 per cent larger than the final 3-D size you want. Finally, draw a long piece that will form the top of the head and nose of your dog. This should widen in the middle and needs to be the same length as the top edge of the side of the head.

3. Now cut out the paper designs and use them as patterns to cut pieces of fabric. For each foot, the sides of the head and the tail, remember to cut two pieces for each, reversing the pattern for one, if your fabric has a 'good' side.

4. A nice way of using up smaller scraps for the body of your dog is to sew together lots of narrow strips of fabric until you have the required length. After sewing all the strips, press the seams flat at the back. Then cut a longer strip to run along the whole length of the sausage and up the back to the place where the tail will be. You will sew this strip on later, while attaching the feet and tail.

5. Next, sew and stuff the feet and tail for your dog. Place the two pieces of fabric with the 'right' side inwards and sew around them 1cm from the edge, leaving the end that will be nearest the body open. Then, turn them right-side out and fill tightly with your stuffing up to within 2cm of the top.

6. You can now sew up the body of the dog. Start by pinning the central 'stomach' strip to one side of the main body with the 'wrong' side outwards. Leave enough of the stomach strip free at one end to go up the back of the dog to its tail, and incorporate the ends of two of the stuffed feet into this seam at the appropriate places (make sure they are placed inside – which will be the outside of the dog – and that the feet are facing forwards). Sew this seam, then repeat at the other side, incorporating the other two feet into the seam.

7. Now you can sew up the back of the dog. Keeping the sausage inside out, bend the strip of stomach material around and pin it to the end of the body. At the top, where the three pieces of material meet, add the stuffed tail and sew everything together with strong stitches.

8. Turn the body the right way out and you can move on to making the head. Start with the ears. Place the two sides of each ear together with the right sides inwards and sew around the seams, leaving the inside edge open. Then turn them the right side out. You will want the ears to be floppy, so don't add stuffing, simply cut a piece of upholstery wadding to the same shape and place this inside.

9. Next, put the head together. Pin the ears into the two seams that run along the top of the head, where the top strip meets the side. Sew these seams, then pin the bottom part of the two sides together, up to the nose.

10. Before sewing this seam, it's a good idea to turn the head the right way round and check the dog's face will have the shape and character you want. You can make adjustments to change the shape of the nose by changing the position of this seam. Once you're happy, sew it up.

11. This is the time to add the eyes and nose. Where you put these will make a big difference to the final character of your dog, so it's a good idea to partly stuff the head before deciding on the correct position. Once you know where these places are, mark them with a pencil, remove the stuffing and snip tiny holes for the posts of the eyes and nose. From the inside, fix on the safety washers (these are designed not to be removed, so be careful that you get the placement right first time).

12. The next step is to stuff the head and body of your dog. The fabrics I used to cover my dog were pale, and there were some dark shades mixed into the stuffing materials, so I added a layer of white upholstery wadding inside the head and body before putting in stuffing. If you have used thicker or darker material for your dog, you won't need to do this.

13. The head should be stuffed firmly, but for the body, you can add as much or as little stuffing as you like. The dog needs to have some bulk to block drafts, but the overall firmness is up to you.

14. When the body and head are both nearly filled, attach the head to the body at the back of the neck by sewing a seam inside. Then, continue adding stuffing to the final parts of the neck and body, while gradually adding more stitches from the outside to close the gap.

15. Continue adding stuffing and stitches until you have completely closed up the seams at the bottom of the neck.

The best stitch to use for this final stage is 'slip stitch', this involves picking up a small amount of fabric from each side of the seam in turn, then pulling the seam together. This forms a neat line and leaves the stitches almost invisible.

See the project on page 138 for how to make a shade like this one, from an old map.

5

Love your lamps

Love your lamps

A lamp is a very simple electrical appliance. With no moving parts, apart from a switch, you can transform or create a lamp from ready-made fittings without any special skills.

When reclaiming electrical fittings, safety is obviously important. When buying second-hand, you can be fairly confident your lamp will be safe – any professional merchant is required to check and test items before reselling. However, private internet sales and 'free-cycling' are not very well regulated so, if you are ever in doubt about the safety of a lamp you want to work on, always ask an electrician to check the wiring.

This chapter shows how to revamp two very different chandelier fittings that I found outside a house that was being renovated. One has been repainted in a plain, bright colour, the other decorated with a range of reclaimed ribbons and beads from charity shops and craft stores.

I also show you how to turn a vintage enamel shade, a block of builder's wood and an empty olive oil tin into bases for lamps. It's especially rewarding to see how easy it can be to transform almost anything into a unique light fitting, provided you can make or use a hole to attach the bulb holder.

I then demonstrate how to re-cover lampshades with a variety of materials, including old maps, wallpaper and fabrics.

Making a new lampshade from an old frame is probably the project with the highest ratio of effect to effort in this whole book. Any suitably sized piece of card, paper or fabric can be used to give a completely new look to your lighting, with just a couple of hours and simple techniques that anyone can master.

Lamp bases

Almost any piece of junk with a bit of height and weight has the potential to be the base for a lamp. The circuitry isn't complicated: a plug, wire, lamp socket and switch are all easy to fix together with a screwdriver and attach to your project.

If this daunts you (or if regulations mean you can't use self-wired lamps in your workplace or home), you can buy ready-to-use lamp kits, which simply fix on the top of a base.

For these projects, I've made three different pieces of junk into lamps: an old French enamel hanging lampshade, a block of wood from a building site and an empty olive oil tin.

The basic steps for each project are the same. Simply make (or use) a hole at the top for the lamp fitting, make another smaller hole at the bottom for the cable to come out, then decorate the base, add the electrics and fix on a shade.

What you'll need
A tall pendant lampshade
Pliers
Electrical tape or duct tape
Lamp fitting, wires, switch and plug
Screwdrivers
Shade and shade support
Lightbulb

Vintage enamel lampshade
1. As this base used to be a lampshade, a lamp socket will fit perfectly into the existing hole at the top, with no work needed.

2. At the bottom, to allow a cable to pass under the edge, use the cutting edge of a pair of pliers to snip a small flap and bend the metal inside the lamp. Use electrical tape or duct tape to cover any sharp edges so they don't cut at the cable later.

3. Finally, add a switch and a plug to the lamp fitting cable, then attach a shade support, lightbulb and shade. And turn the power on.

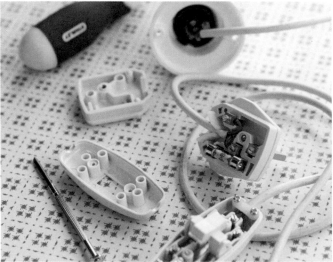

Wooden block

This block of wood was left over from building a school near my home. I thought it would be great if it was made to look like the base of a mushroom, to complement my vintage lampshade. So, I carved away the corners and left the finish rough, using woodstain and oil for a deeper colour.

1. To fit the wires through the block, drill two holes – one from the top and one from the side, aiming both holes at an angle so they meet up in the middle. Getting this right involves a bit of trial and error, but any mistakes you make inside the block won't be visible. Draw pencil lines on the side of the block to help get the angles right. When you know the holes are close to meeting up, use a slow drill speed and move the drill around in the hole until you break through.

If you are using a ready-wired lamp kit, you need to drill only one large hole in the top of the lamp, then carve a channel around to the back of the lamp for the cable.

2. To round off the block and create an attractive carved surface, use specialist wood carving tools (easy to find at good hardware stores). With a curved tool, angle gently into the wood and use a hammer to carve off small chips until you have the shape you want.

3. To finish off the base, wipe on wood stain with an old rag until you get the right colour. Then, add two applications of Danish oil and, when they have soaked in, buff gently with a clean rag.

4. Now you can add the electrical fitting. Push the cable through the hole, leaving spare length at either end to complete the wiring. I chose a plastic lamp socket designed to be screwed downwards onto the base.

5. Add the shade support, lightbulb and lampshade.

Olive oil tin

This decorative tin of olive oil had a hole at the top for a pouring spout, which was perfect for a lamp fitting. With an empty tea tin used as a shade, it makes an ideal kitchen lamp.

What you'll need

Empty olive oil tin
Pointed nose pliers
Screwdriver and hammer
Lamp fitting, wires, switch and plug
Clear silicone sealant
Beads, sand or pebbles
A small spoon
Small screws
Shade support
Empty tin of tea
Tin opener
A drill and a small drill bit
suitable for metal
Lightbulb

1. Start by pulling out the plastic spout from the olive oil tin using pliers. Then, clean the inside thoroughly by filling with hot water and detergent and shaking vigorously. Repeat this several times until all the oil residue has gone, then leave the tin somewhere warm to dry.

2. To make a hole for the wire at the bottom of one of the sides, use a flat screwdriver and hammer to punch through the tin, then bend the sharp edges inside with pointed pliers.

3. To add weight for stability, and prevent the lamp from being top-heavy, you'll need to part-fill the tin with beads or sand. I used sand, so the hole at the bottom needed to be sealed to stop it leaking out. To do this, I wired on the lamp fitting to the end of the cable, pushed the cable through the empty tin, then used clear silicone sealant to fix the wire in place and plug the hole.

To make a good seal, push plenty of silicone through the gaps between the cable and the tin, then smooth around the cable on the outside with a soapy finger before leaving it to dry for several hours.

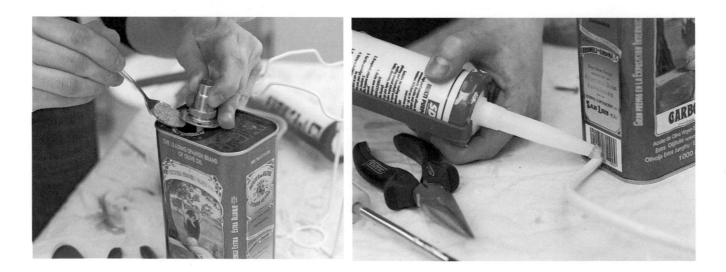

4. Once the sealant has set, you can spoon beads, sand or pebbles through the top hole until you have enough weight inside to prevent it tipping over easily.

5. Now you can finish off the wiring. Secure the lamp fitting to the top of the tin with small screws (these will go straight into the tin without pilot holes) and add a plug. Make sure the plug has a low fuse rating for a small lamp like this.

6. To hold the shade, you will need to add a shade support, and this will need to be trimmed to the correct height. Measure up your tea tin, so that the bulb in the fitting will be fully surrounded, then snip off the posts of the shade support with pliers.

7. Next, prepare the tea tin. This kind of tin is ideal for a small lampshade because it comes with a round hole at the top. All you need to do is remove the bottom with a traditional tin opener, press down any sharp edges with pliers, then drill a few small holes with a metal drill bit to let light through.

8. Finally, place the tin on top of your lamp and add a bulb. Low-energy lightbulbs are best when you are using a shade made of metal because they give off very little heat.

Reclaimed chandeliers

These two metal light fittings (one hanging chandelier and one three-armed lamp that fits directly onto the ceiling) were thrown out onto the street when a house near me was being refurbished. They were very scuffed and scratched, and not exactly the height of fashion.

However, after checking the wiring, it looked like they were still in working order, so I took them home, tested them and treated them to a brand new look – one with a bright paint job and the other with beads and ribbons.

Safety note – electrical items

If you're not sure a reclaimed electrical fitting is safe to wire in, always get a qualified electrician to check and test it for you. There's every chance a lamp will have been thrown away for cosmetic reasons, but you can never be too careful. Check your local regulations too, in case DIY electrical work is prohibited. If so, help from a professional is essential.

Painted chandelier

Hanging lights can look a bit heavy in black or dark metallic shades. Why not give them a more contemporary feel with a bright zing of colour, such as this deep blue?

What you'll need

Metal chandelier

Wire wool

Masking tape

Enamel or gloss paint

Paint brushes

Newspaper or a dust sheet

Spray paint

White spirit (to clean brushes)

Lightbulbs

Getting an even coat with spray paint can be tricky if you're spraying a complex shape like this, so try my two-stage method using a brush to reach the tricky parts, then following up with spray paint in a slightly brighter shade. This gives the appearance of a really deep coloured finish.

1. Clean the metal parts of the chandelier and rub all over with wire wool to remove any loose paint and rust.

2. Protect the lamp sockets and wires with masking tape before starting to paint.

3. With enamel or gloss paint and a small brush, paint a thick base coat all over the whole chandelier, paying particular attention to any hard-to-reach places that the spray may miss. A good method is to do this in several stages, turning over the chandelier each time and painting all the surfaces you can see from each angle until they have all been covered.

4. Once the enamel is thoroughly dry, protect the area with newspaper or a large sheet, and add a second coat with spray paint. To reduce the chance of spraying too thickly and causing drips, hold the can about 30cm from the lamp and, again, work in stages to spray from every angle.

5. After the spray paint is dry, all you need to do is remove the masking tape, hang and wire it in, and add lightbulbs.

Lamp decorated with beads and ribbons
This lamp (shown overleaf) would look great in a bedroom or dressing room. I've painted it in matt white, then decorated with a range of beads and ribbons and added reclaimed glass shades.

What you'll need
Lamp (see photo)
Wire wool
Masking tape
Radiator paint or enamel in matt white
Ribbons, beads, bangles, old necklaces and any other decorations you can find
Thin craft wire
Replacement lampshades (optional)
Sponge (optional)
Specialist glass tinting paint (optional)

1. Clean the metal parts and rub down with wire wool.

2. Wrap the plastic lamp fittings in masking tape before painting.

3. Brush all over with matt white enamel or specialist radiator paint (this paint is very good for using on metal). Add several coats to build up a thick, tough layer of white paint with a flat white finish.

4. Once dry, add beads in any arrangement you like. Attach necklaces and strings of beads to the posts by wrapping long pieces of craft wire around several times, before twisting the ends. Craft wire is ideal for attaching beads securely to a lamp such as this. Because the posts have a thick coat of paint, it is even less likely to slip down or come loose later.

5. When you are happy with the arrangement of beads, add ribbons, tying them around the posts to cover the places where wires are attached, then let them hang down.

6. At the top of the fitting, near the ceiling rose, a thicker piece of ribbon is a good way to cover up the ends of the necklaces and any untidy wires.

7. Finally, add the shades. I put gold-coloured bangles under each of mine before screwing on, and also put more bangles inside the clear glass shade. (This is safe if the lamp fitting is made of plastic as there is no danger of the bangles coming into contact with live parts of the circuit.)

I tried out three different ways of replacing or revamping the glass shades on this lamp. I found two amber coloured glass shades in a junk shop, and used one of these in its original clear state. The second of these I painted inside with white paint. This makes a really interesting effect when used with coloured glass, as the shade of the colour changes subtly with the thickness of the glass.

If you want to try this, dab the paint inside the glass with a sponge, so that brush marks won't show through when the lamp is lit.

Lastly, I re-used one of the original frosted glass shades, painting the inside yellow with specialist glass-tinting paint, from a craft shop.

A new lampshade from old

Revamping a lampshade is a quick, easy and very satisfying project, and you can use almost any reclaimed paper or fabric junk.

With this old map of Paris, I've made a small square shade and a large cylindrical shade, which I've added to the enamel lamp base from page 126. The metal frame of your shade may have a different shape than the one I've used here but the basic process for any lampshade revamp follows the same steps.

Safety note – Fireproofing
It's important that your lampshade materials are resistant to fire. All your finished lampshades made from paper and fabric should be sprayed with a special 'fireproofing spray' before use. You can buy this spray from most hardware suppliers. Sprayed lightly onto your finished shades, it will make sure they don't easily catch fire.

For another example, see the fabric-covered shade I made to put on the metal lamp stand on page 19. This used exactly the same technique, but with fabric taken from an old blouse glued onto card before stitching onto the frame.

What you'll need
Old lampshade
A large sheet of medium-weight card
Pencil
Sharp scissors
Paper or fabric large enough to cover the shade
Iron
Dust sheet
Repositionable spray glue
Needle and thread
Bias tape or other trim
Clear glue, suitable for fabrics

1. Before taking apart your old shade, use it to measure the card for the new one. The best way to do this is to place the shade on the card and roll it along, drawing a pencil line along the edge. If your shade is cone shaped, roll it around in a curve and draw a line along both edges. Add 2cm at the end to allow for overlap and cut out the card.

2. Take the paper or fabric you want to use for a new cover and press it to remove any creases. Then, using the card as a template, cut it out slightly larger than the card all around.

3. Place the card on a dust sheet and spray it lightly all over with glue. Place the paper or fabric on top and smooth it down. Using repositionable spray glue allows you to make adjustments for a short time if you make any creases. Once the glue is dry, trim the paper around the edges of the card.

4. Now, remove the old lampshade covering from the frame. You will probably end up with two separate metal parts, one with a support ring attached.

5. Roll up the new shade cover and ensure it correctly fits around the top part of the shade.

6. Now you are ready to stitch the card onto the shade. Start with the top part, sewing it onto the frame with a simple looping stitch known as 'overstitching'. Repeat this process with the bottom ring.

7. Fix the seam where the card overlaps with clear glue, applying it from the inside of the shade so the glue doesn't leak out.

8. To finish off, cover up the stitching at the top and bottom of your shade with bias tape. Apply clear adhesive over the stitches on the outside and around the metal frame. Wait for this to dry slightly before pressing the bias tape around the edge. Repeat this at the bottom. Simple tape looks neat and attractive, but you can glue or stitch a more decorative trim around the edges if you prefer.

6

Trade and office leftovers

Trade and office leftovers

**Many home renovation tasks will result in spare materials
left behind to clutter up the loft or cellar, and these can
be a rich source of ideas for clever new projects.**

In this chapter I've used laminate flooring strips to make a modular wine rack, bricks to
make a bookshelf and an old printing block to make a door wedge. And don't forget the
flooring rubber used in the previous chapters to make a garden table and placemats.
This was left over from a friend's bathroom renovation, but has helped to make my
house much better too, since I've used it for several very different, and useful, projects.

Office chuck-outs offer opportunities for free or cheap items. Many useful, decorative
or unusual things can result from large renovations and end up being left out with the
rubbish. If you ask the supervisor or manager nicely they are very likely to let you take
these items home to re-use them. I've even made a circular canvas for a painting by
pulling stretchy denim around part of a revolving door from an office building that was
undergoing a major refurbishment.

Desks and filing cabinets are more commonly discarded by workplaces having a clear-
out, but these don't always look very homely. In this chapter, I show how to transform an
ugly metal filing cabinet into something much more attractive for your home using fabric,
paint and real wood veneer.

I've combined painting, fabric and wood coverings in just one project here, but any one
of these techniques used alone could give a new look to similar office furniture, so a filing
cabinet revamp doesn't have to take a long time to complete.

Wine rack from leftover laminate

There are usually a few spare laminate strips left over from laying a floor. This project re-uses some of these to make a simple wine rack.

About 2.5 metres of 20cm wide laminate is enough for this rack. If you have more pieces to play with, cut extra parts to the same designs for a flexible 'wine rack kit' that can be fixed together in different arrangements.

What you'll need

Laminate flooring strips
Tape measure or ruler
Pencil
Tenon saw (or a jigsaw to save time)
Masking tape
Small chisel
Hammer
Rough sandpaper

1. Measure the thickness of your laminate pieces (mine were 5mm thick) and add 1mm to get the correct width for the slots.

2. Mark up the laminate ready for cutting. For my design you will need four pieces 40cm long, with slots placed at 2, 11, 20, 29 and 38cm, and four pieces 22cm long, with slots at 2, 11 and 20cm (measurements are to the centre of each slot). Each slot should reach about halfway across the strips. My slots were 6mm wide and 10cm long.

3. Next cut the long edges of all the slots using a large tenon saw or jigsaw. If using a jigsaw, use masking tape to hold the free edge down when cutting the final slot, or support it with another piece of board, placed underneath. If left free, the vibrations from the power tool may cause the thin final strip of material to break off.

4. Cut through the short edges of the slots using a small chisel and hammer.

5. Remove the strips of material from the slots and sand any rough edges. Make sure the laminate will fit into all the slots. If any are too tight, widen them with folded pieces of rough sandpaper.

6. To construct your wine rack, simply push the pieces together to make a diagonal pattern of squares. Line up the slots at right angles, making sure the wood-patterned surfaces are all facing upwards, then knock each piece gently into place.

Junk Fiends: Peter Martin

Everyday junk is what inspires Peter Martin. He's even invented a new type of bottle top as part of his mission to reduce the waste involved in the products we use in our daily lives.

'The things I do with junk are unlikely to get into *Vogue*,' says the founder of the Junkk website, where waste-reducing ideas are shared and swapped by people from all over the world.

'The ideas I like best aren't gorgeous, just practical ways of re-using ordinary things in the home. My background is in science and engineering, but my career is in advertising, and what really fires me up is persuading people to look at things differently and come up with new ideas.

'I've never liked waste. My mother was a good Scots lady. From her I learned that you don't throw things out, and the Junkk site is all about that. It's been online for thirteen years, and has always been a kind of social network for garbage, allowing people to exchange information about how they have re-used items.

'The site now has thousands of ideas and questions, covering everything from coasters made from shoelaces to jewellery made from aluminium cans. If you have a neat idea for re-use, it's simple to add it. And if you want a neat idea, it's easy to find it.'

By including space for the exact measurements of items, the site's database is carefully designed to make matching up questions and answers easier, and has led to some unusual ideas being put forward. One of the most creative is Peter's own creation, the 'Vac Sac'.

'Looking at a broken vacuum cleaner, the plastic body seemed ideal for a sturdy, lightweight backpack. So I removed the inner parts, lined it, fitted it up with leather straps and found it worked perfectly.

I want it to become a commercial project. However, the first prototype was battleship grey and too sober-looking to catch people's attention, so I made it shocking pink with red fur straps and the Junkk logo on the side. That really helps to start conversations when I take it to trade fairs!'

'It's a bigger idea. What if we designed things to be re-used, rather than having ideas only after they have become junk? Why not build the next function into the product in the first place?'

Peter also wants to see more things manufactured with re-use in mind. His invention, the 'RE:tie' was inspired by seeing the strips used as seals for juice bottles (known in the industry as 'tamper-evident security closures') lying around littering the streets. Peter could see how much the strips resembled small cable ties and had the idea that, if they could be redesigned, they wouldn't be thrown away but kept as a useful little 'gift' from the drinks company.

'I worked at it for a while, and then patented a new design for the strip and had some made. It doesn't use more plastic, tearing the strip off the bottle is actually easier with the redesigned tab, and the change to the manufacturing process in the factory is as simple as swapping one mould for another.' Despite winning prizes, no manufacturer has yet been persuaded to change their bottle design to use the RE:tie, but Peter is hopeful his idea will catch on.

'People love it to death, and there are so many companies seeking to prove their green credentials that I can't believe it won't be taken up very soon.'

Decorated filing cabinet

Some furniture from the office looks great as it is. A wooden filing cabinet, desk or a neutral shelving unit can be bought cheaply (or even be free) when businesses refurbish their offices. Such items can be cleaned up and used straight away in the home if they are in good condition.

I found a large black metal filing cabinet in a second-hand office supplier, but it was too dark, boxy and formidable to use without some work. My revamp uses real wood veneer, paint and reclaimed kimono fabric to make an attractive piece of storage for a home study.

1. Start by cleaning and preparing the cabinet. Scrub down the surfaces with wire wool to provide a good surface for painting.

2. Special radiator paint is great for a job like this, which needs to be tough and resistant to scratches. It dries almost without leaving any brush marks, and two thin coats are enough for a resilient finish.

What you'll need

Metal filing cabinet
Wire wool
Radiator paint
Paint brushes
A sheet of wood veneer
A sharp craft knife
Contact adhesive
Rubber printing roller
Fabric
Measuring tape or ruler
Scissors
Iron
Newspaper and masking tape
Spray glue
Clear glue, suitable for fabrics
Waxed card from food packaging
Spray paint and acrylic or emulsion in bright colours to match the fabric
Sponge
Sandpaper
Wood filler
Acrylic varnish

Veneer is very fragile but, if pieces do break apart, you can glue them closely together with an almost invisible join. Any gaps or chips can be filled with wood filler before varnishing.

3. Covering the top surface with wood veneer helps to soften the boxy look of the cabinet. Use a craft knife to cut pieces to fit the upper and side surfaces of the top part of the cabinet from a sheet of veneer, bought inexpensively from a specialist supplier. Glue it on with contact adhesive, spreading a thin layer of glue onto the cabinet and leaving until it is nearly dry before pressing on the veneer. I also used a small rubber printing roller to make sure the veneer was pressed hard onto every part of the surfaces.

4. Next, add fabric to the drawer fronts. I found some reclaimed fine woollen kimono fabric on an internet auction site and its bright pinks and oranges look gorgeous next to the pale purple paint on the rest of the cabinet.

5. Cut the fabric into pieces slightly larger than each drawer front and press it to remove creases. Then, protect the drawer handles and the rest of the cabinet with masking tape and newspaper before spraying a thin layer of spray glue onto the front panels. Place the fabric carefully and press it down with your hands from the centre to the edges.

6. Finish off the drawer fronts by trimming the fabric to within 1cm of each edge, folding around the sides and sticking down with clear glue.

7. I thought that the large flat sides of my cabinet also needed decoration, so I copied some of the motifs from the fabric pattern onto waxed card, cut out stencils and used fluorescent orange spray paint to add bright flowers. Before spraying, make sure again to protect the rest of the cabinet with newspaper and masking tape.

8. After the spray paint has dried, you can add more stencilled motifs in other colours using more spray paint or acrylic or emulsion paint. When using liquid paint, avoid drips and runs by applying a thin layer using a sponge.

9. To finish off the wooden top of the cabinet, sand gently at the corners (which will be sharp where two thin strips of veneer meet). Then, fill in any gaps and seams between pieces with wood filler and sand this down smooth as well.

10. Finally, add a few coats of acrylic varnish to seal and protect the wood.

Stencil tips

Any kind of waxed card can be used to make a stencil. It's important to use something non-absorbent, so your stencil can be re-used several times. I used the packaging from a supermarket meal, which was perfect for the job.

Use a really sharp knife to cut out the pattern, and don't forget to add 'bridges' to your design wherever an outline is needed, or the central shapes will fall out!

To get a clear edge, it helps if the stencil sticks to the surface. For this, use a thin layer of spray glue on the back of the stencil. This gives just the right amount of 'stick' and allows the stencil to be peeled away after painting.

Door wedges made from scrap wood

Unless you live on a spaceship with sliding doors, your house will certainly need a door wedge or two. Why buy these when you can make them from any wooden off-cuts left over from home or office improvements?

I've used a piece of door frame and some scraps of wooden planks (left over from making shelves for my brick bookcase on page 160) to make two wedges that also use up other junk – an old printing block and a leftover tile.

What you'll need

Scraps of wood (any will do, as you can glue them together before cutting out your wedge shape)

PVA (wood or craft) glue

Masking tape

Saw

Sandpaper in various grades and sanding block

Wood stain and Danish oil

Rags

Tiles, printing blocks or anything else that's square and decorative to put on the top of the wedge

1. If you are using smaller scraps of wood, first make a block suitable for cutting out a wedge by gluing them together. Use wood glue and wrap the pieces tightly in masking tape while the block dries. This will give a really strong bond.

2. Now cut your wedge shape using a saw and holding the block in a vice or work bench. A very shallow angle of about 15–25 degrees is best, so that your wedge will fit snugly under a range of doors. Leave a suitably sized flat surface on top for your decorative item.

3. Sand the whole thing smooth, starting with rough sandpaper and ending with a fine grade.

4. Using stain and oil for this project is better than varnish because the finished wedge will be scraped by door edges when in use. If you want the wedge to be darker apply stain to the bottom and sides of the wedge with a rag then add two applications of oil to soak right into these surfaces. Don't forget to leave the flat top surface oil-free, so the glue for the final stage will stick firmly. When the oil is dry, buff with a clean rag.

5. To finish off, use wood glue to stick down your printing block or tile.

Office storage made from covered boxes and floppy disks

When my office bought a batch of new computers, we ended up with a large number of packing boxes in lots of different shapes and sizes.

Covered with paper, I've turned these boxes into a handy storage and filing system for my writing desk at home.

I've also made a cute pen holder from some old floppy disks, held together with cable ties.

What you'll need

A range of cardboard boxes

Craft knife, or kitchen knife and scissors

Sugar paper or wrapping paper
in co-ordinated colours

PVA (wood or craft) glue

Spare card

Water-based varnish (optional)

Brushes for glue and varnish

Duct tape (optional)

Office storage

1. Use the craft knife or kitchen knife to cut your boxes to the shapes you need. Cut a slot in the front of a flat box to make an 'in tray', or take a corner off a tall box for a magazine tidy.

2. Cover each box with paper. Wrap them as if they were a birthday present, folding down the flaps to make neat corners and then gluing these down.

3. For the inside bases and sides of boxes, cover a flat piece of spare card with paper and glue this inside, covering any untidy edges that have been folded into the box.

4. If your wrapping paper is pale in colour or delicate, add a coat of water-based varnish to protect it and create a longer-lasting finish.

5. Now stick the boxes together in a suitable arrangement. You can use glue for this or, if the back of your arrangement will be against a wall, a quicker method is to use strips of duct tape.

Desk tidy from floppy disks

These floppy disks were in a box of old college work. Turning them into a desk tidy saves them from gathering dust in a cupboard, but doesn't ruin them. So, if I ever need to look at my microscope pictures again, I can simply snip the cable ties and put the disks back into a computer that has a suitable drive.

What you'll need
Five floppy disks
Masking tape
Drill and small wood drill bit
Small cable ties
Small, sharp scissors
(nail scissors are ideal)

1. The disks have holes at two of the corners already, which are ideally placed for adding cable ties, but you will need to add two more holes.

   Drill all the disks at once by taping them tightly into a block with masking tape. Then, use a small wood drill bit to add holes to the remaining corners. These holes will be a long way from the data disk inside, and creating them should not damage the disks. However, if the data is very precious do copy it onto a computer first.

2. Remove the tape then construct the sides of the box by putting cable ties through the adjacent corners, making sure the closures end up inside the box. Attach the closures, but don't pull the ties fully tight yet.

3. When all four sides are joined together, add the base using the same method. Some of the ties will need to go through the same holes you already used to hold the sides together.

4. With all the parts of the box shape in place, you can now tighten the cable ties. Do this gradually, pulling each one tighter in turn and making sure the edges are lined up neatly at each stage.

5. When the ties are all pulled tight, snip off the free ends of the strips inside the box, using small, sharp scissors.

Bookshelf made from bricks

Exposed bricks can look very chic when used indoors. Here I've used them to support reclaimed planks and display some books and ornaments.

Rather than use messy (and heavy) cement, I have found a quicker and easier way to create the brick stacks by using expanding filler.

What you'll need
Reclaimed bricks
Plastic sheet
Expanding foam filler
Saw
Emulsion paint and paint brush
Masking tape
Reclaimed planks
Sandpaper in various grades
Danish oil and old rags

It's a good idea to arrange all your stacks of bricks at the same time. Line them up so they can be squeezed and nudged into place to exactly match in height and prevent your bookshelf from being wobbly.

1. Clean up the bricks and leave them slightly damp. This helps the filler to stick to the surfaces.

2. Place a plastic sheet on the ground and lay the sets of three bricks on top of the sheet. Then shake the can and spray a small amount of foam filler into each gap.

   The filler expands rapidly and, after about a minute, will start to push the bricks apart, so it's a good idea to squeeze the bricks together slightly after this time so that each stack continues to line up with the others. It will also ensure that the filler grips every part of the surfaces.

   Don't worry about the amount of filler spilling out – this gets removed in the next step. The foam filler takes about 24 hours to set properly. After this time, peel the brick stacks off the plastic sheeting to reveal one perfectly 'mortared' side.

3. On the other sides, there will be excess filler that needs to be removed. The material is incredibly light and easy to cut, so you can simply slice it off with an ordinary saw.

4. You can buy filler in a few different colours (mainly shades of yellow and green), but the surface does look a bit plastic. For a better colour, and for a more cement-like appearance, paint the filler with a suitable emulsion paint, protecting the bricks with masking tape.

I got my bricks from an architectural salvage yard. They're from an old fireplace and are slightly smaller than house bricks, but any kind of brick can be used for this project. Larger bricks, and higher stacks, can be used for bigger books.

5. Next, prepare the shelves. I cut mine from panels of the reclaimed door used for the tiled table on page 84. Use rough sandpaper to smooth down the surfaces, then finer sandpaper to polish it ready for oiling. A quick couple of applications of Danish oil (see page 23) and your bookshelf is ready to be put together.

6. Stack the shelves and bricks together in a suitable arrangement. When you are building more than one layer, the stack won't be perfectly stable unless it has some support, so the best place for these shelves is an alcove or corner.

Because nothing is fixed together (apart from the stacks of bricks) these shelves are very flexible and can be taken apart and rearranged as many times as you like. This method is also ideal for filling a nook or alcove with a more complex, taller arrangement of shelves and bricks.

Kid's stuff

KID'S STUFF

**Making toys from empty bottles and boxes was a big part
of my childhood. Now, as an adult, I have been having almost
as much fun being creative with junk to make things for children.**

I have used a wide variety of materials in this chapter, from bathroom bottles and tin cans, which you might find in your recycling bin, to bike parts begged from my local repair shop. Two separate projects have come from taking apart an old rocking horse that was left out in my street. I've rearranged and re-used the different parts to make a doll's house and a wall clock.

You can complete some of these projects with the help of children, who will love the chance to decide on the final colours and decorations for the mobiles, wall clocks, doll's house and kit bag. Some could even be completed alone by older children, or by younger children under close supervision. The simple magic trick wallet project is ideal for children to have a go at themselves, and is quick and easy enough to complete in one rainy afternoon.

There's more involved in making a doll's house or a kit bag, with steps such as sewing a strong seam, screwing hinges or cutting out window holes. Some of the potentially dangerous tools needed for these projects, such as needles and saws, are definitely best kept away from young hands. However, your children could still help to decorate and finish off these projects after you have done the main work of putting the pieces together.

They can also safely join in with some of the fun (and messy) ways of making items for mobiles, such as moulding a papier mâché planet!

A MAGIC TRICK WALLET

This is a classic homemade toy, which is a perfect project for making with recycled materials.

It's a simple but effective trick called a 'magic wallet'. The pieces of card joined with ribbons can be opened from both sides. So, if you place an item beneath the ribbons, then close and (secretly) flip the wallet, when it's opened again the item will appear to have moved to the other side by itself! I've used packaging card and ribbon from gift-wrapping to do this, but any flat, strong ribbon-like material will work.

This project is also safe to make with your child, especially if you do all the cutting out beforehand.

What you'll need

Two thick pieces of card approximately 10cm by 6cm in size (these need to be plain or have a pattern that is not 'directional', so cover them in paper if needed)

Two pieces of matching ribbon, about four times the width of your card

Paper or wood (PVA or craft) glue

Two pieces of thick paper, or thinner card for the 'cover' of the wallet

1. Take your plain pieces of card and lay them next to each other on a table. The sides that will form the cover of the wallet should be facing upwards.

2. Glue the ends of the ribbons close to the top and bottom of the left-hand edge of the card on the left side. Leave the glue to dry.

3. Now wrap the ribbons neatly around the cards as follows:

 • Straight across around the back of the left-hand card

 • Straight across over the front of the right-hand card

 • Diagonally, crossing over in the middle, across the back of the right-hand card

 • Out through the gap between the cards onto the front of the left-hand card

4. When the ribbons are all trained correctly and neatly around this path, pull gently to bring the cards close together, then trim the ends and glue the ribbons in place wherever they contact the upper surfaces of the card (don't glue anything on the underside).

5. To cover the glued ends of the ribbons, stick the thinner pieces of card or paper over the outside cover of the wallet.

JUNK MOBILES

Rooms for children should be full of bright, interesting things and that shouldn't stop at the ceiling. Moving around in the breeze, mobiles can be educational, inspirational, fun or simply pretty, and provide a great opportunity to utilise small items of junk.

Many of these projects can be made with your child's help. However, remember to keep young children away from sharp knives and scissors and to let them work on the other jobs only under close supervision. Attaching the final pieces to wires and balancing the different parts can be quite a delicate task, so this is probably best done by you.

Here I've made mobiles with bars made from twigs and wires, and used images from the internet, reclaimed bottles and tins and books to make items for hanging. I've also made an educational mobile from an old board book. I hope the range of materials I've used will inspire you to see the potential of many more pieces of junk to be used in similar projects.

Constructing the frame of a mobile

What you'll need
Stiff wire, twigs or any 'stick' material that can have string attached securely at the ends without slipping off
Pointed nose pliers (for wire mobiles)
Drill (if needed, for thicker sticks of wood)
Items for hanging
Strong thread, twine, fishing line or string for attaching bars and items

1. For a wire mobile, prepare the horizontal bars by cutting pieces of wire (using the cutting edge of pliers) to different lengths, then gripping the ends firmly with pointed nose pliers and bending small loops. If you find that the loops at either end do not point in the same direction, grab each end with a pair of pliers and twist until they line up.

2. Using twigs for the bars can look very attractive. Try to cut the ends where there is a natural 'bulge' or side branch that will stop the string from sliding off. Make sure the twigs can hold the weight of the items you want to hang. For these mobiles, it's probably best to stick to very light materials, such as the paper and card shapes I've used on the following pages.

3. When you have finished your bars and items for hanging then you are ready to start putting the mobile together.

4. The key to a successful mobile is to make sure the different items are balanced, make a good overall shape and don't bash into each other when they move around in the breeze. One method of building up a good shape is to start with a large item at the top of the mobile. This will be attached directly to the hook in the ceiling, and the rest of the mobile will hang down from it.

5. For the next layer, add a bar with items hanging from either end, or put an item at one end and a string leading down to another bar at the other.

6. You can hang further bars from the ends or centres of the bars in each layer and build up the shape from there. Keep adding more items until you have a shape that looks good, balances and moves around freely.

7. Another important consideration is how the strings are attached to your items. Ideally, the items should be allowed to spin, so hang them from a single piece of string or twine, which can twist in the middle. Or place a double loop of string through a small ring attached to your item to allow it to twist and turn.

Board book mobile

What you'll need
A small board book with large pictures
Sharp craft knife
Drill or hole punch
Eyelet kit, with punch
Hammer

1. Cut the board book into individual pages using the craft knife. Trim any rough edges then make large holes at each corner, strengthening each hole with an eyelet.

2. Eyelets are available in kits from haberdashery shops (they are intended for repairing belts) and come complete with a small tool that closes the eyelet tight around the material.

Printed images on card mobile

1. A wealth of copyright-free, public domain images are available online, taken from books and paintings whose artists have died long ago.

   When you find a good image, like this lovely picture of flower fairies, save it then use an editing program to make two versions – one flipped horizontally so that they can be used to stick to the back of each piece of card.

2. Print several copies of each version, then stick them to both sides of some pieces of lightweight card. To line up the images exactly, push pins through the card at significant points in the design and match these up.

3. Then, cut out particular elements from the images using a craft knife. For the top of my mobile, I used the whole central part of the picture, then I cut out separate items from other copies for pieces to hang from the rest of the mobile.

4. Use a hole punch to make a neat hole in each piece for the thread. Hung from bars made out of twigs, this mobile is unique and very pretty.

A bathroom bottle balloon mobile

What you'll need
Empty spherical bottles of shower gel
(or hollow plastic toy balls)
Pointed punch or bradawl
Small key-rings
Empty 'travel size' shampoo bottles
Fabric
Needle and thread
Small coins

1. Novelty shower gel bottles gave me the idea of making a mobile of small hot air balloons. You could use any hollow plastic ball.

   To hang up the balloons, and to make sure they can spin freely, make two holes in the top of each ball with a punch or bradawl and attach a key-ring.

2. The bottoms of small shampoo bottles are a good shape to make baskets for these balloons. To hang them, add a notched circle of fabric to the top of each ball and use a needle and strong thread to attach the baskets to the circles.

   Because the plastic baskets are very light, a few small coins added to each one adds weight to make them hang better.

A space-themed mobile

What you'll need

Plastic robot

Ball

Wallpaper paste

Newspaper (for papier mâché)

Brushes for paint and paste

Tiling grout

Watercolour paints

Empty bottle

Piece of paper

Bottle tops

Empty tin

Metallic paint

Jar top

Scrap of wood

Screws and screwdriver

1. For this mobile, I made and collected a random set of space-related items. I found the plastic robot in a charity shop, then made a moon by covering a ball in papier mâché and tiling grout, painting on craters with watercolours.

2. I created the rocket out of an empty bottle of wood glue, painted white with a paper nose cone and a collection of plastic bottle tops stuck together on the bottom for engines.

3. The satellite is simply an empty tin painted silver on the outside and blue on the inside. I added the top of a jar and a scrap of wood, attached with screws, to make a radio dish and a solar panel.

A DOLL'S HOUSE MADE FROM A ROCKING HORSE

I brought home the broken rocking horse shown on page 7 with the aim of repairing it. However, it didn't rock smoothly so, after seeing an old doll's house in a museum, I had the idea of taking it to pieces and using the parts in a different arrangement as the basis for a completely new toy.

I've re-used a range of other junk in the course of this project. The base is the door of a kitchen cupboard, while the central wooden wall is from a panel of the oak door used to make the tiled table on page 84.

Inside, I've made a kitchen stove from scraps of hardboard, a mirror from food packaging and a bath from the end of a takeaway dinner container.

Designing a doll's house
The important thing about a doll's house is that it should be easy for a child to play with and simple to redecorate it when they want.

That's why I designed mine not just with a removable front panel, but also with sides and a back that all fold down, making it easy to move dolls and furniture around, and to clean, repaint and add more accessories, such as curtains, in the future. Using magnetic or ball catches to hold things together means there are no fiddly moving parts to break off or catch little fingers.

What you'll need

Old rocking horse

Some new hardboard and plywood for larger parts, such as the roof, front and back walls

Measuring tape

Wooden scraps, boards and posts

Screwdriver

Wood glue, screws, saws, chisels, sandpaper and other woodworking equipment

Primer and paint

Paint brushes

Drill

Four strong hinges

Magnetic or ball catches

Yogurt or cream pot lid

Craft paint

---

1. Starting with the roof, and taking the rocking horse runners as the basic shape, add four struts made from other parts of the rocking horse, then cut a piece of hardboard to fit over the top. Screw the hardboard carefully in place, bending it around the curves.

2. Cut a hole for a chimney next to one of the roof struts. From another scrap of wood, cut a post and drill holes in the end before putting it through the hole and screwing it onto the strut.

3. Sand, fill and prime the edges and screw holes in the roof, then paint with two coats of black gloss.

4. Next, make the sides of the house. For this, the legs of the rocking horse were ideal. Cut the four pieces to the correct angle for the side walls (so that the top edge is narrow enough to fit snugly under the roof), and attach them to the door frame base with hinges.

   Enclose the side walls with hardboard pieces, attached with screws and wood glue. Before fixing these in place, cut holes for windows and use more wooden offcuts to surround the holes. This ensures that, when the hardboard is attached around the sides, the windows have frames inside.

   This method of making the side walls ensures that they look solid, but are very light.

5. Cut pieces for the front and back walls from new plywood (or use scrap materials if you have pieces large enough). Cut holes for a door and windows in appropriate places.

6. The back wall should be fixed to the base with a hinge, and held up against the walls with magnetic catches, or ball catches, when closed. Screw the catches in place after fixing the hinges.

7. The front wall can be completely removed for playing. When closed up, it needs to sit in a slot in front of the side walls. Cut this slot with a saw and chisel and check the front wall will sit flat against the sides.

8. The central walls of this design are also removable. They fix to each other with a simple pair of slots – similar to the method used for the wine rack on page 144. You will also need to cut slots in the side walls to support the ends of the upper floor.

9. Now all the basic construction work is finished, the floor, base, sides, and the front and back walls can be sanded smooth, primed and painted, ready for the really fun part: the final decorations.

10. You can finish off your house in any style you like. For mine, I added window frames made from rough strips of wood, glued together and painted green before gluing to the walls (gluing rather than nailing on these small parts ensures that if they do break off during rough play, there won't be any sharp metal parts sticking out).

    I also painted leaves and glued fabric flowers around the front door, and used pieces of decorative strip wood for skirting boards on the inside. The walls and floors were also painted in different colours and designs for each room.

11. For a final decorative touch, make a front door from two pieces of hardboard with semicircular holes cut out, and sandwich the pieces around an already painted piece of plastic cut from the top of a pot of cream or yogurt. Use special clear craft paint for this job, in order to get an authentic stained glass effect.

FABRIC KIT BAG

The pattern for this kit bag is so easy it can be sewn by hand or machine, even if you have limited skills with a needle. One long cord makes a drawstring closure at the top and two handles for carrying over the shoulder.

For the body of my bag, I've used strong cotton material and plaited my handles from long strips of fabric from an old curtain.

What you'll need

Two rectangular pieces of fabric

Sharp scissors

A piece of strong, thick cord four times the length of the material

Needle and thread, or a sewing machine

Large safety pin or button

1. Start by cutting out two matching rectangles of material. Place these next to each other on a flat surface with the 'wrong' side upwards.

2. Work out how wide the channels across the top of each side need to be for your cord to slide through comfortably. The easiest way to do this is to fold the fabric over the cord. Remember to allow for the seams when doing this. Snip the fabric about 1cm in from each side at a point just below this. Fold the sides in at the top and sew four short hems in the sides above the cuts you have made (these will help stop the ends of the fabric from fraying when the cord is pulled through the channels).

3. Now fold down the top edges and sew two seams to make the channels for the cord.

4. Next, place the two sides of the bag together with the 'right' sides facing inwards and sew the side seams, leaving the bottom open.

5. To add the cord, start by placing it inside the bag (still with the 'right' sides facing inwards). Place one end of the cord so that it is poking out of the bottom of the right hand corner next to the seam, and sew diagonally across this corner a few times to fix it in place.

6. Pull the other end of the cord out of the bag at the top and thread it through the backmost channel from right to left (it can help to attach a large safety pin or button to the end of the cord before pulling it through). When it emerges at the other end, thread it back through the front channel, this time from left to right.

Why not make a waterproof version of this bag for swimming kit, using material cut from a worn-out raincoat?

7. Once the cord has been threaded through both channels, put the free end back inside the bag and pull it down so that it pokes out of the bottom right corner, next to the first end that was fixed in place. Sew across it diagonally another few times (it's important that the cord is attached securely to the bag at this corner).

8. Now you can finish off the bottom seam, turn the bag right-side out and you're finished.

CREATE A CLOCK

A clock mechanism kit can be used to reclaim many different items. They are inexpensive and often sold specifically for making a clock from a CD or vinyl record. These are good junk ideas already, but you can be more inventive and build clocks out of many other leftover items.

Here are two clocks I have made for children's bedrooms: one from the rocking horse's head left over from the doll's house project on page 176; the other made from parts of old bicycles.

What you'll need
Pencil

A piece of sheet wood or board

Jigsaw or hacksaw

Drill

Sandpaper and sanding block

Primer

Paint brushes

Water-based gloss paint

Any other decorations your child wants to add

Clock mechanism kit (buy one with a spindle long enough to fit through your piece of wood)

Horse head clock
My horse's head came ready-made but, using a jigsaw or hacksaw, any scrap of sheet material can be cut into a similar shape.

This project is also ideal for finishing off with your child's help if you use water-based non-toxic paints for the final stage.

1. Draw and cut out your shape using a jigsaw or hacksaw. Clamp the piece firmly and work in short stages for safety. If you are using a hacksaw, cut any curves in a series of straight lines. These curves will need quite a lot of smoothing off later.

2. Drill a hole in a suitable place for the centre of your clock.

3. Sand the edges of your cut-out shape smooth, then add a coat of primer.

4. When the primer is dry, sand it lightly and you're ready to paint the final coat.

5. Add a base coat, then either leave the clock as a plain shape or ask your child to help decorate it with stickers or patterns, or to add other decorations.

6. Once dry, simply attach the clock mechanism through the hole, tighten the nut and hang it up.

Bike-gear clock

This pedal and hub was abandoned in a litter bin. The central hole was too deep for a clock spindle, so I asked my local repair shop for some more worn-out bicycle parts that I could combine with it to make an interesting design.

1. Used bike parts are likely to be very oily, so scrub them clean with strong household detergent to give a good surface for painting on.

2. Spray paint is the easiest way to cover these fiddly shapes. Working outside, spread out some newspaper or a dust sheet on the ground and prop the parts up on bricks or scraps of waste wood. Then spray several coats from different angles until every part is covered. Use different colours for each part, or leave some bare for an attractive combination.

3. The parts are not likely to need to be glued together. For my clock, I wedged the flat circular gears firmly into the gaps between the chain rings in the main hub, then put the clock spindle through one of the holes where they overlapped and tightened the nut to hold things in place. Use epoxy resin glue if you need to fix together parts that can't be attached this way.

4. This clock will be quite heavy. Hang it up with picture wire attached to the metal parts, rather than using the plastic hook that is part of the clock mechanism. Put it on a strong hook, fixed securely into a door or wall.

For materials that are much thicker than a CD, look online for non-standard mechanisms with longer spindles. Items up to around 20mm thick can be converted using these kits.

Resources and useful information

Junk Fiends
Dave and Debbie Powell
Visit the Bracknell Re-use Project website at:
www.bracknellreuseproject.co.uk

Hilary Bruffell
Find more great ideas and initiatives from the Make It and Mend It team at: **www.makeitandmendit.com**

Peter Martin
Add your own re-use ideas to the database at **www.junkk.com**

Gabrielle Treanor
See more of Gabrielle's creations at:
www.thegreengables.co.uk

Finding junk
Often, the best bargains are not found at large, famous antique and vintage markets, but at independent local junk shops and charity shops selling second-hand furniture. Look these up in local newspapers, or in online directories, such as **yell.com**.

UK
Charity shops:
Find a directory at: **www.charityretail.org.uk**
www.bhf.org.uk - British Heart Foundation
www.oxfam.org.uk/shop - Oxfam
www.pdsa.org.uk - PDSA
www.suerydercare.org - Sue Ryder

Salvage and reclamation yards:
Find a directory at: **www.salvo.co.uk**
www.stoneagearchitectural.com
www.lassco.co.uk
www.bygones.net
www.fromerec.co.uk
www.beestonreclamation.co.uk

Junk, vintage and antique furniture:
www.salvo.co.uk – this site also lists second-hand shops, as well as salvage and antique reclamation stockists.

www.bada.org – the British Antique Dealers' Association has a director of dealers and details of fairs and markets.

www.antiques-atlas.com – this site also gives details of hundreds of antiques fairs and dealers across the UK.

www.portobelloroad.co.uk – Portobello Road is the world's most famous antiques market, with street stalls selling bargains, as well as dealerships housed inside dozens of arcades and shops.

USA/Australia/World
Freecycle.org
This site matches up unwanted items and good homes in local areas around the world to help everyone reduce waste. Find your local group and register to look for items available close to you.

ebay.com
The original online auction site, where you can find almost literally anything for sale, and often at a bargain price. A wide range of second-hand, junk and vintage shops also maintain online shops here, with international shipping available, and it's a great place to start your search, especially if you want something unusual.

craigslist.org
A online classified advertising site that is rapidly expanding to cover most of the world. Its 'for sale' section contains furniture, household items and craft categories, and you can restrict the search to your own region or town.

gumtree.com
A network of sites, covering six countries, carrying online classified adverts that include plenty of inexpensive furnishings and household items that are ripe for revamping.

www.salvoweb.com
This website covers the USA, France, Australia, Canada, UK and many other locations around the world. It lists reclamation yards, dealers in antiques and vintage furniture and fabrics, and a range of second-hand shops where you can find quality junk items.

Suppliers of tools and materials
When you need advice on materials and equipment to complete a tricky junk project, your local suppliers will also often have the best value and the most personal service. For tools, specialist supplies and hardware, these online suppliers will deliver to your home and have a very wide range of products that cover all the different techniques used in *Junk for Joy!*

UK
Tools, hardware and materials:
www.screwfix.com
www.toolsonline.co.uk
www.diy.com
www.ironmongerydirect.co.uk
www.wickes.co.uk
www.buildbase.co.uk

Wood veneer products:
www.capitalcrispin.com
www.originalmarquetry.co.uk
www.selectveneers.com

Electrical and lamp fittings:
www.maplin.co.uk
www.ryness.co.uk

Fabric, sewing and upholstery supplies:
www.johnlewis.com
www.sewessential.co.uk
www.jamiltonupholstery.co.uk
www.upholsteryshop.co.uk
www.upholsterywarehouse.co.uk
www.cutfoam.co.uk
www.foamcut2size.co.uk
www.efoam.co.uk
www.bandmlatexupholstery.co.uk
www.smfoam.co.uk

Craft supplies:
www.the-beadshop.co.uk
www.fredaldous.co.uk
www.craft-supplies.co.uk
www.regalcrafts.com

US/Australia/World

Electrical and lamp fittings:
www.1000bulbs.com – USA and international shipping.

Fabric, sewing and upholstery supplies:
www.fabric.com – USA-based supplier of all things related to fabrics and sewing.

www.vintagefabrics.com.au – Australia-based supplier of vintage fabrics, including swatch packs and scrap bags.

www.petitjapon.com – vintage and second-hand kimonos and fabrics from Japan.

www.vintagepretty.com – specialising in picking out quirky and unusual vintage fabrics.

www.ragrescue.co.uk – smaller pieces and scrap-bags cut from pretty vintage materials from around Europe.

Craft supplies:
www.etsy.com – stockists of handmade items from an international range of craftspeople, as well as vintage materials and supplies.

www.aussiecrafts.com.au – with a store locator for independent suppliers within Australia.

www.craft.com.au – Australian craft superstore with almost every kind of tool and material.

Advice and information on techniques

This book gives detailed advice on the particular projects I have carried out for my home, but your own junk may have different characteristics and you may need to adapt or find new techniques to complete a project. The internet is a great place to start when you have a problem like this to solve. Often you will find a helpful person halfway across the world has posted a video or step-by-step guide covering exactly what you need to find out!

Worldwide
www.threadbanger.com – an archive of original videos covering a wide range of sewing projects and repairs.

www.craftzine.com – Craft magazine's US-based website with ideas on a wide range of crafts and renovations.

www.instructables.com – videos and step-by-step tutorials on everything from cooking to kissing, this site also has a vast selection of DIY and craft tips.

www.wikihow.com – a collaborative 'how to' manual for the world. Not always reliable on techniques (the users submit their own advice) but still a good source of ideas.

www.ehow.com – another huge site of household tips, including some great craft and homewares projects.

Index

Bold items – full projects
Italic numbers – important or full-page illustrations of projects or materials, when not on same page as the project itself